# The Struggle for Equality: Landmark Court Cases

**Lucent Library of Black History**

Stephen Currie

**LUCENT BOOKS**
*A part of Gale, Cengage Learning*

GALE
CENGAGE Learning

Detroit • New York • San Francisco • New Haven, Conn • Waterville, Maine • London

GALE
CENGAGE Learning™

© 2010 Gale, Cengage Learning

LIBRARY OF CONGRESS CATALOGING-IN-PUBLICATION DATA

Currie, Stephen, 1960–
  The struggle for equality : landmark court cases / by Stephen Currie.
    p. cm. -- (Lucent library of Black history)
  Includes bibliographical references and index.
  ISBN 978-1-4205-0122-3 (hardcover)
  1. African Americans--Legal status, laws, etc.--Cases--Juvenile literature.  I. Title.
   KF4757.C868 2009
   342.7308'73--dc22
                                                      2009010781

Lucent Books
27500 Drake Rd.
Farmington Hills, MI 48331

ISBN-13: 978-1-4205-0122-3
ISBN-10: 1-4205-0122-4

Printed in the United States of America
1 2 3 4 5 6 7 13 12 11 10 09

# Contents

Foreword                                                    4

**Introduction**
African Americans and the Courts                            6

**Chapter One**
The *Dred Scott* Decision                                  10

**Chapter Two**
*Plessy v. Ferguson*                                       25

**Chapter Three**
*Brown v. Board of Education*                              41

**Chapter Four**
Voting Rights and Political Power                          59

**Chapter Five**
Affirmative Action                                         74

Notes                                                      91
For More Information                                       96
Index                                                      99
Picture Credits                                           103
About the Author                                          104

# Foreword

It has been more than 500 years since Africans were first brought to the New World in shackles, and over 140 years since slavery was formally abolished in the United States. Over 50 years have passed since the fallacy of "separate but equal" was obliterated in the American courts, and more than 40 years since the watershed Civil Rights Act of 1965 guaranteed the rights and liberties of all Americans, especially those of color. Over time, these changes have become celebrated landmarks in American history. In the twenty-first century, African American men and women are politicians, judges, diplomats, professors, deans, doctors, artists, athletes, business owners, and home owners. For many, the scars of the past have melted away in the opportunities that have been found in contemporary society. Observers such as Peter N. Kirsanow, who sits on the U.S. Commission of Civil Rights, point to these accomplishments and conclude, "The growing black middle class may be viewed as proof that most of the civil rights battles have been won."

In spite of these legal victories, however, prejudice and inequality have persisted in American society. In 2003, African Americans comprised just 12 percent of the nation's population, yet accounted for 44 percent of its prison inmates and 24 percent of its poor. Racially motivated hate crimes continue to appear on the pages of major newspapers in many American cities. Furthermore, many African Americans still experience either overt or muted racism in their daily lives. A 1996 study undertaken by Professor Nancy Krieger of the Harvard School of Public Health, for example, found that 80 percent of the African American participants reported having experienced racial discrimination in one or more settings, including at work or school, applying for housing and medical care, from the police or in the courts, and on the street or in a public setting.

It is for these reasons that many believe the struggle for racial equality and justice is far from over. These episodes of discrimination threaten to shatter the illusion that America has completely overcome its racist past, causing many black Americans to become increasingly frustrated and confused. Scholar and writer Ellis Cose has described this splintered state in the following way: "I have done everything I was supposed to do. I have stayed out of trouble with the law, gone to the right schools, and worked myself nearly to death. What more do they want? Why in God's name won't they accept me as a full human being?" For Cose and others, the struggle for equality and justice has yet to be fully achieved.

In many subtle yet important ways the traumatic experiences of slavery and segregation continue to inform the way race is discussed and experienced in the twenty-first century. Indeed, it is possible that America will always grapple with the fallout from its distressing past. Ulric Haynes, dean of the Hofstra University School of Business has said, "Perhaps race will always matter, given the historical circumstances under which we came to this country." But studying this past and understanding how it contributes to present-day dialogues about race and history in America is a critical component of contemporary education. To this end, the Lucent Library of Black History offers a thorough look at the experiences that have shaped the black community and the American people as a whole. Annotated bibliographies provide readers with ideas for further research, while fully documented primary and secondary source quotations enhance the text. Each book in the series explores a different episode of black history; together they provide students with a wealth of information as well as launching points for further study and discussion.

# Introduction

# African Americans and the Courts

The story of African Americans through history has in large part been the story of prejudice and discrimination. Until the Civil War, most American blacks were slaves, forced to labor for no pay and subjected to beatings and other punishments for all manner of offenses, real and imagined. When slavery was abolished, blacks still were denied political and economic power; their voting rights were sharply limited, their job prospects were poor, and their children were required to attend substandard schools. Only toward the end of the twentieth century did African Americans, as a group, begin to approach the social and economic status of whites.

Through most of this time, the laws of states and the federal government were not on the side of America's blacks. Slavery, after all, was perfectly legal in every southern state until 1865— and throughout the Northeast, as well, during colonial times and beyond. The slave system was inhumane and immoral, but it had the power of the law behind it. Later, it was the law, not simply tradition, that kept blacks from voting and barred African American children from attending schools built for whites. All across the country, for most of American history, lawmakers at all levels of government have passed legislation designed to keep blacks poor and powerless.

But though individual laws have not often favored African Americans, the legal system itself has often been the best hope for America's black population. This apparent contradiction has to do with the workings of American government, which consists of three branches, or parts. One part is the legislative branch—Congress, in the case of the national government—which makes the laws. Another part is the executive branch, led by the president at the national level. This branch is responsible for carrying out the laws—for making sure they are followed. These two branches are in the news constantly, and it is easy to think of them sometimes as making up the entire government. However, they do not.

The third branch of government, known as the judicial branch, consists of America's courts. The court system determines guilt or innocence in both criminal cases—that is, those that have to do with people who commit crimes—and civil cases, in which people or governments file lawsuits against one another. For years, one of the functions of the judicial branch has been to interpret the laws—to determine what the laws actually mean. In particular, the courts are sometimes asked to decide if a particular law is in keeping with the U.S. Constitution, the document that sets the framework for all the laws in the country.

**The court system has the vital function of interpreting the U.S. Constitution in regard to the law.**

The judicial system, thus, wields plenty of power. Courts have the final say in the legal process. They have the authority to overturn existing laws, and they can also interpret laws in ways that legislators never intended. This power has sometimes been used to the detriment of blacks—but not always. Indeed, some of the most important gains made by African Americans through the years have come about as a result of decisions by federal courts. And whether the decisions have been favorable to blacks or not, no one questions that court rulings over the years have significantly shaped the course of African American history—and the history of the nation as a whole.

## The Court System

The federal government has its own civil court system; the states have their own as well. Most cases brought between citizens or corporations within the same state begin in state court. Cases in which the participants are from different states, however, more often begin

in federal court. The person who files the lawsuit is known as the plaintiff, and the person defending the suit is the defendant. Case names use the form *Plaintiff v. Defendant*, where the letter *v* stands for *versus*, or *against*. In *Plessy v. Ferguson*, for example, the plaintiff, Plessy, brought suit against Ferguson, the defendant.

The court system resembles a pyramid. Most cases start in a small, low-level court. The court—a term also used to stand for the judge or judges who preside over the case—hears testimony from lawyers for both sides. The judges study the laws that seem to apply, review the facts of the case, and then issue a ruling. Often this ruling is based on precedent, or how earlier, similar cases have been decided. Most low-level

**The U.S. Supreme Court has the final say in any court case, and its rulings cannot be overturned except by itself.**

courts use a panel of judges, usually three. Whichever side the majority of the judges supports is the winner.

The first court is not necessarily the only one to hear the case, however. The loser in the case can sometimes file an appeal, or ask to move the case to a higher, or more powerful, court. To file an appeal, the loser of the suit must argue that the initial ruling was flawed in some way, whether because proper procedure was not followed or because the verdict was based on an incorrect reading of the law. Simple disagreement with the ruling is not grounds for appeal. If an appeal is made, the higher court reviews the case and the initial decision. It can choose to overturn or uphold the earlier decision—that is, it can reject the verdict or accept it. Again, the loser may have the option to appeal to the next level.

There is an end to this pyramid of courts, though, and that is the U.S. Supreme Court. This court cannot be overruled; the decision of its nine members, known as justices, is final. The Supreme Court often creates the precedents that courts look to in deciding new cases. The Court's justices take pains to explain their reasoning in great detail. They write essays known as opinions, which tell how they interpreted each case and list the laws that they believe apply. Justices may write opinions of their own, or they may join in the opinions of other justices who agree with them. These opinions are called dissents when they go against the opinion of the majority.

The courts, then, are a significant and critical part of the American system of government. Together with laws passed by Congress and the states and actions taken by presidents and governors, the decisions of judges have been instrumental in shaping American life in general—and the lives and fortunes of African Americans in particular.

## Chapter One

# The *Dred Scott* Decision

**B**etween the early 1800s and the outbreak of the Civil War in 1861, the most significant issue that faced Americans was the question of slavery. Embraced in the South and forbidden in the north, slavery separated the regions and threatened the unity of the nation. Arguments that appealed to antislavery forces seemed naive and dangerous to those who supported the institution; at the same time, southern defenses of slavery struck northern opponents as misguided and evil. Slavery came to underlie debate over everything from economic policies to westward expansion.

It is no surprise, then, that slavery was at the root of *Scott v. Sandford*, one of the most important Supreme Court cases of this period. On the surface, *Scott v. Sandford* seemed innocuous enough. The question was whether Dred and Harriet Scott, both of them born into slavery, were legally free after having lived for several years in the north. But the case proved much more complex than it appeared. Political considerations and legal principles alike led to a ruling that went far beyond the original scope of the case and affected the status of nearly every African American in the country. Cheered by some and denounced by others, the *Dred Scott* decision, as it came to be known, helped push South and North further apart—and helped bring about the Civil War.

## Dred Scott

Dred Scott, the central figure of *Scott v. Sandford*, was born in Virginia in either 1799 or 1800. His mother was a slave, which made Scott a slave as well. As an early Virginia statute put it, "All children born in this country [that is, Virginia] shall be held bond [enslaved] or free only according to the condition of the mother."[1] Both by custom and by law, then, Scott was a slave from the moment of his birth.

The *Dred Scott* decision was one of the most important Supreme Court cases of its time.

Little is known about Scott's early years. In 1830, however, Scott's owners left Virginia for St. Louis, Missouri. Missouri, like Virginia, was a slave state, and Scott went with them. About a year later, Scott was sold to a St. Louis doctor named John Emerson. At first, Scott worked for Emerson at Emerson's home in Missouri. But in 1834 Emerson took a position with the U.S. Army and was assigned to a post near present-day Rock Island, Illinois.

## Legal Complications

That assignment should have presented a dilemma for Emerson. Like other northern states, Illinois was a free state; that is, it did not allow slavery. In the words of Illinois' constitution, "Neither slavery or involuntary servitude shall . . . be introduced into this state."[2] Nor did Illinois recognize the rights of slave owners who brought their slaves into the state. The law, then, was clear: Scott could claim his freedom if he moved to Illinois with his master.

But Emerson brought Scott with him regardless. Perhaps he believed that Scott had no interest in becoming free. Slave owners often attributed such feelings to their chattels; many were shocked when their supposedly happy slaves ran off as soon as they had the opportunity to do so. Or perhaps Emerson assumed that the people of Illinois would not support Scott if he did seek his freedom. Certainly Illinois was not friendly to African Americans, and while Illinoisans did not particularly care for slavery, most had no strong objection to it either.

In any case, Emerson moved to Rock Island and brought Scott along. For the next two years Scott lived as a slave in a free state. There is no indication that he tried to assert his freedom during this time, nor is there any sign that he attempted to escape. Neither did anyone at the fort or in the nearby town intervene on Scott's behalf. And in 1836, when Emerson was transferred to the post of Fort Snelling in present-day Minnesota, Scott went too.

## States and Territories

Minnesota, at that point, was not yet a state but a part of the Wisconsin Territory. A territory was a lightly populated possession of the United States. Several such territories were near Illinois and Missouri; Kansas, Iowa, and Arkansas, for example, were all U.S. terri-

This map of the United States shows the division of the country into slave and nonslave states, as prescribed by the Missouri Compromise of 1820.

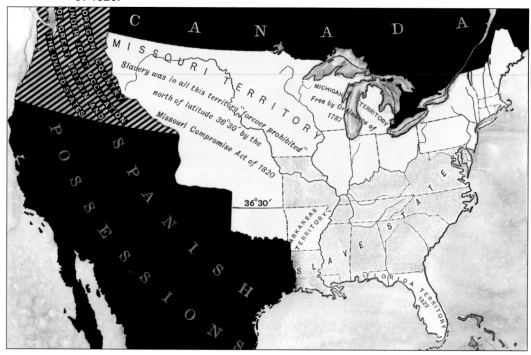

# The Missouri Compromise

━━━━━━━━━━━━━■━━━━━━━━━━━━

In the early 1800s, long before the Civil War, the institution of slavery more than once threatened to split the nation. The most important of these threats arose in 1820, when the slave territory of Missouri applied for statehood. Missouri had enough people to become a state, but northerners objected. The number of slave states at that time precisely equaled the number of free states, and northerners did not want to tip that balance in favor of the South. However, no free territory was populous enough to join the Union.

The two sides argued bitterly for months, and some politicians wondered if civil war would be the result. In the end, though, lawmakers passed the Missouri Compromise. Under this law, Missouri was admitted as a slave state, and present-day Maine was broken away from Massachusetts to balance it. The Missouri Compromise also settled the question of slavery in other territories, banning slavery north and west of Missouri, while allowing the institution in the Arkansas Territory to the south.

Violence had been averted; the compromise was satisfactory to both sides. But Thomas Jefferson suspected the calm would not last. "[The conflict] is hushed, indeed, for the moment," he wrote. "But this is a reprieve only, not a final sentence."

Quoted in Allan Nevins and Henry Steele Commager, *A Pocket History of the United States*. Sixth edition, New York: Pocket Books, 1976, p. 162.

tories at this time. During Dred Scott's childhood, lawmakers had debated the question of whether slavery should be allowed in these possessions. In 1820 they settled the issue with a law known as the Missouri Compromise. One provision of this law banned slavery north of an imaginary line extending west from Missouri's southern boundary. As the compromise stated, "Slavery and involuntary servitude [shall be] forever prohibited"[3] for this region.

Minnesota was considerably north of this boundary line, and so slavery was forbidden within its borders. Yet once again, Emerson apparently had no hesitation in taking Scott to Minnesota. Nor was Scott the only slave at Fort Snelling. A government employee in the area, whose home was also in the South, had brought along a young slave named Harriet Robinson. Although Harriet was only about half Dred's age when the two met in 1836, they soon married, and Emerson purchased Harriet from her former owner.

## Filing Suit

In 1837 Emerson was reassigned again, this time to a post in the slave state of Louisiana. He left the Scotts in Fort Snelling, where they worked for other military officers. These officers paid Emerson for the use of his slaves, but the Scotts got nothing other than food and a place to sleep. Dred and Harriet spent most of the next three years in Minnesota, interrupted only by a brief trip to Louisiana soon after Emerson met and married a woman named Irene Sanford. Finally, in 1840 the Scotts returned to St. Louis, this time for good.

Three years later John Emerson died. The Scotts, together with their two young daughters, now became the property of Irene Emerson, John's widow. Life with Irene Emerson, however, did not suit the family. Dred tried to gain their liberty by purchasing

The Old Courthouse in St. Louis, Missouri, was the site of one of the *Dred Scott* trials.

it from Mrs. Emerson, but she refused. In 1846 the Scotts turned to the courts. Each filed suit against Irene Emerson, asserting that their years on free soil had made them free. They charged her with false imprisonment, and they demanded their freedom.

Under Missouri law, the Scotts were entitled to file suit. Although slaves had few rights in Missouri, as in the rest of the South, the state did allow slaves to sue for their liberty. "Any person held in slavery," read a statute passed in 1824 and still in effect more than two decades later, "may be permitted to sue . . . stating the ground upon which his or her claim to freedom is founded."[4] Indeed, Missouri law gave African Americans every opportunity to prove that they were unjustly held in slavery. The law even assigned the slave a lawyer at state expense if he or she had no money, as most did not.

## Earlier Cases

Legal precedent was on the Scotts' side, too. Missouri courts took seriously the claims of slaves who argued that they were free by virtue of having lived on free soil. The first such case was *Winny v. Whitesides*, which came before the state supreme court in 1824. Phebe Whitesides had lived in Illinois for several years with her slave Winny and Winny's children. When Whitesides and Winny moved to Missouri, Winny sued for her freedom. The court found for Winny and her children and released them from bondage for good.

Other Missouri cases followed, strengthening the principle that extended time in a free state gave slaves their freedom. In the 1837 case of *Wilson v. Melvin*, a southerner stopped in Illinois for a month while bringing his slaves from Kentucky to Missouri. Upon arriving in Missouri, one slave sued for his freedom. The master clearly did not intend to settle in Illinois. But the court ruled that the real question was "whether the master made any unnecessary delay in Illinois with his slaves."[5] The judge decided that the stay on free soil had not been necessary and awarded the slave his freedom.

Another Missouri case, *Rachael v. Walker*, had particularly strong connections to the Scotts' situation. An army officer had taken his slave, Rachael, to Fort Snelling—the same place where Dred and Harriet had met and married. When she returned to

Missouri several years later, Rachael sued for her freedom. Her owner argued that the military had assigned him to Fort Snelling. He had gone there because those were his orders, he explained, and he argued that he should not lose his property for doing what he was told. The court rejected that argument, however, and directed that Rachael be freed.

Under these circumstances, it is likely that the Scotts and their lawyers expected an easy victory. State courts had already ruled, after all, that being a military officer did not exempt a slave owner from the need to follow the law. And Dred and Harriet Scott had spent most of the previous four years on free soil—considerably longer than the one month in Illinois that gained the plaintiff in *Wilson v. Melvin* his freedom. As one modern commentator writes, "The Scotts' claim appeared to be open and shut."[6]

## Ups and Downs

But it was not. The trial got off to a rocky beginning for the Scotts. As slaves, the Scotts could not testify in court, so they had to establish in other ways that they had lived in free territory. Accordingly, the Scotts' lawyer called several witnesses to testify on their behalf. The witnesses agreed that the Scotts had lived on free soil. They also established that the Scotts had once been the property of John Emerson.

There was a problem, however. As it turned out, none of the witnesses had direct knowledge that Irene Emerson now owned the Scotts. Since the Scotts' case had been brought against Irene Emerson, that left a large hole in their argument. Without evidence that Irene Emerson was the Scotts' owner, the jury was unable to rule in their favor. The court denied the Scotts' petition and returned them to the custody of—bizarrely enough—Emerson herself. "The decision," writes historian Don Fehrenbacher, "had the absurd effect of allowing Mrs. Emerson to keep her slaves simply because no one had proved that they were her slaves."[7]

The Scotts were discouraged but not defeated. Several years later they asked the judge for a second trial, and their request was granted. When the new trial began in 1850, the Scotts were prepared with a new lawyer—and new witnesses. These witnesses established not only that the Scotts had lived in Minnesota but

A 1958 reenactment of the *Dred Scott* trial shows two lawyers arguing the case with a gallery of black and white spectators behind them.

that Irene Emerson was now their owner. This time, the jury decided in the Scotts' favor.

But the case was not over. Irene Emerson appealed the verdict to the Missouri Supreme Court. And though she had no new arguments on her side, she did have an unexpected advantage. A major political change was under way in the United States, a change that would affect the way judges and juries thought about the Scotts—and about slavery itself.

## Another Verdict

Since 1840 the debate over slavery had become increasingly intense. Both northerners and southerners were growing more and more aggressive in expressing their views. This was perhaps especially true in the South. Once, southerners had been slightly embarrassed by their institution. They had called it a necessary evil, and they had agreed to keep slavery out of most of the territories. Now, however, they were going on the attack. Southern leaders praised slavery as a positive good, and they demanded that slavery be allowed in all U.S. territories. Most important, perhaps, they began to view any attempt to limit slavery, however small, as a direct attack on the South.

This political perspective affected Missouri as much as any other slave state. Increasingly, proslavery Missourians argued that their state should disregard other states' laws against slavery. They saw no reason why Missouri should accept the antislavery sentiments of northerners who did not seem to have the South's best interests at heart. By the time Emerson's appeal came to the state supreme court, many of Missouri's leaders felt this way. That list included two of the court's three judges.

The appeal was heard early in 1852, and the result was a 2–1 victory for Emerson. The court noted that its ruling stemmed largely from the new political climate. "Times now are not as they were when the previous decisions on the subject were made,"[8] remarked Justice William Scott. It would be foolish indeed, Scott argued, to recognize the antislavery laws of Illinois or Minnesota given the growing northern hostility to slavery. "The inevitable consequence [of this hostility]," Scott added, "must be the overthrow and destruction of our Government. It does not behoove the State of Missouri to [submit] to any measure which might gratify this spirit."[9]

## Another Attempt

The decision was a terrible blow to Dred and Harriet Scott. But it still did not end the case. Soon after the ruling, Irene Emerson put the Scotts under the care of her brother, John Sanford, who lived in New York. While the Scotts had used all their options under Missouri's legal system, they could file suit in a federal court if their case was against a person who was a citizen of another state. Because Sanford did not live in Missouri, the Scotts' attorneys now sued him in the federal courts. The case came to trial in April 1854.

During the trial, lawyers for Sanford (whose name was misspelled as *Sandford* in court documents) brought up a new argument. They asserted that the Scotts had no right to sue. Only citizens could file suit, they told the court, and the Scotts were not citizens. Indeed, the Scotts could not be citizens, even if they were not slaves, the attorneys said, because their race disqualified them. "Dred Scott is not a citizen of the State of Missouri," explained one attorney, "because he is a negro of African descent."[10]

Though a slaveholder himself, the judge, Robert Wells, rejected this argument and allowed the suit to go forward. In the end, however, Wells ruled against the Scotts. Missouri's supreme court had ruled that slaves remained slaves even after living in the north, and Wells felt forced to accept that interpretation. The decision was not his personal preference. "My feelings were deeply interested in favor of the poor fellow," he wrote afterward, "and I wish the law was in favor of his freedom."[11] Despite his wishes, though, the Scotts remained enslaved.

## The Supreme Court

One option remained: an appeal to the U.S. Supreme Court. The Scotts' attorneys suspected, however, that this option would fail. Of the nine justices on the Supreme Court, five were southerners who supported slavery. Two of the northern judges strongly opposed federal interference in the affairs of individual states, and the Scotts' attorneys expected these two men to accept the Missouri court's ruling too. But despite this apparent lack of support, the Scotts' attorneys nonetheless filed an appeal late in 1854.

More delays followed. It was 1856 before the Court began to hear arguments in the case. Sanford's lawyers repeated their earlier contention that the Scotts were not citizens and therefore had no right to sue. They also argued that the right of Missourians to own property—in this case, slaves—could not be displaced by laws in Illinois or elsewhere. Finally, they challenged the Missouri Compromise itself. Congress, they claimed, had no right to forbid slavery in the territories. Thus, the ban on slavery in Minnesota was void. The Scotts could not assert their freedom.

The Scotts' lawyers countered each argument. They repeated their opinion that the Scotts were citizens of both Missouri and the United States. They pointed out that Missouri courts had traditionally ruled in favor of slaves who had lived in free states. And they asserted that the Missouri Compromise was perfectly legal. For proof, they pointed to Article 4, Section 3 of the U.S. Constitution, which holds that "Congress shall have Power to . . . make all needful Rules and Regulations respecting the Territory . . . belonging to the United States."[12]

## The Verdict

The Court deliberated for several months. After much discussion, Chief Justice Roger Taney issued the Court's official opinion on March 5, 1857. For the Scotts, the news was grim. By a 7–2 majority, the justices agreed that the Scotts were still slaves. The laws of Missouri, they concluded, supported Sanford's case, and these laws were the only ones that counted. Moreover, even if the Scotts had been technically free while they were in the north, their move back to Missouri had made them slaves once again.

But the Court went further. It decided to address the question of citizenship as well. Taney argued that there were two ways to become a U.S. citizen. One was naturalization, or being granted citizenship after emigrating from another country. The other was to be descended from people who were citizens at the time the Constitution went into effect. In Taney's view, that second group did not include African Americans. "Neither the class of persons who had been imported as slaves, nor their descendants, whether they had become free or not, were then acknowledged as a part of the people

Chief Justice Roger Taney issued the Supreme Court ruling against Dred Scott.

# The *Dred Scott* Decision

■

Chief Justice Roger Taney's opinion in *Scott v. Sandford* rejected the validity of the Missouri Compromise. In this excerpt from the decision, Taney explains his reasoning:

> The right of property in a slave is distinctly and expressly affirmed in the Constitution. The right to traffic in it, like an ordinary article of merchandise and property, was guaranteed to the citizens of the United States, in every state that might desire it, for twenty years. And the Government in express terms is pledged to protect it in all future time if the slave escapes from his owner. This is done in plain words—too plain to be misunderstood. And no word can be found in the Constitution which gives Congress a greater power over slave property or which entitles property of that kind to less protection than property of any other description.

Quoted in Maureen Harrison and Steve Gilbert, *Great Decisions of the U.S. Supreme Court*. New York: Excellent Books, 2003, p. 31.

[that is, citizens],"[13] he wrote in his opinion. Under this definition, in fact, virtually no African American could ever be a citizen.

Finally, the Court also took on the issue of the Missouri Compromise. Here, too, the news was bad for those who opposed slavery. "The right of property in a slave is distinctly and expressly affirmed in the Constitution,"[14] Taney argued, adding that Congress could not pass legislation that denied this basic property right. Banning slavery in the territories, Taney reasoned, violated the rights of those who owned slaves. Thus, he concluded, the Missouri Compromise "is not warranted by the Constitution, and is therefore void."[15] Congress, he said, had no power to forbid slavery in any U.S. territory.

Taney's view was not unanimous. Justice Benjamin Curtis was especially vocal in his dissent. He brought up historical evidence to demonstrate that some states had in fact considered African Americans to be citizens before the Constitution took effect. Thus, in his opinion, free blacks could indeed be citizens. Other

# A PUBLIC MEETING

## WILL BE HELD ON

# THURSDAY EVENING, 2D INSTANT,

at 7½ o'clock, in ISRAEL CHURCH, to consider the atrocious decision of the Supreme Court in the

# DRED SCOTT CASE,

and other outrages to which the colored people are subject under the Constitution of the United States.

# C. L. REMOND,
# ROBERT PURVIS

and others will be speakers on the occasion. Mrs. MOTT, Mr. M'KIM and B. S. JONES of Ohio, have also accepted invitations to be present. All persons are invited to attend. Admittance free.

The Supreme Court decision against Dred Scott sparked outrage within the African American community.

justices also took issue with parts of Taney's positions; only two other justices completely agreed with him on the issue of slavery in the territories, for example. But their doubts meant nothing. Taney's decision was the majority opinion, and the case was over.

## Reaction

The verdict infuriated the north's African Americans. Black leader Frederick Douglass denounced the Court's ruling as historically inaccurate and a distortion of the Constitution. Other leaders also made their fury known. "We owe no allegiance to a country which grinds us under its iron heel and treats us like dogs," announced an African American from Philadelphia. "The time has gone by for colored people to talk of patriotism."[16]

But thousands of white northerners were enraged as well. The verdict, many argued, was morally unjust. "If the people obey this decision," editorialized one newspaper, "they disobey God."[17] And the Court's ruling on the Missouri Compromise struck anti-slavery forces as particularly dangerous. If Congress could not keep slavery out of Minnesota or Nebraska, they wondered, did existing free states actually have the right to forbid it? "We shall lie down pleasantly dreaming that the people of Missouri are on

## *Dred Scott* and Modern Scholars

———■———

Few modern scholars have much respect for the Supreme Court's decision in the *Dred Scott* case. Today, experts view *Scott* as poorly reasoned, shoddily researched, and based on political considerations rather than on legal principles. Moreover, historians are deeply critical of the effects of the verdict on African Americans. As a result, this case is among the most extensively criticized of all Supreme Court cases. Historian Harvey Fireside, for example, has called the ruling "the all-time most shameful chapter in U.S. Supreme Court annals."

Modern students of the case criticize several parts of the decision, but the most controversial aspect of the case is probably the Supreme Court's extremely broad ruling. From a judicial perspective, most historians agree that the justices overstepped their bounds in ruling as they did. It was not appropriate, in this view, for the justices to revoke the Missouri Compromise—or indeed to do much of anything other than to determine whether the Scotts were free. Other critics similarly have accused the Court of being more interested in politics than in law. In their eyes, the flaws in the decision stemmed largely from Taney's misguided desire to settle the question of slavery in the territories—a question that should have been left to the president and members of Congress. In any case, the *Scott* decision has few serious defenders today.

Harvey Fireside, *Separate and Unequal*. New York: Carroll and Graf, 2004, p. 7.

the verge of making their State free," warned Abraham Lincoln, "and we shall awake to the reality instead, that the Supreme Court has made Illinois a slave State."[18]

Even northerners who had no strong objection to slavery were distressed. The verdict seemed to give the South the power to dictate policy for the entire country. On this issue, at least, more and more northerners were coming to agree with antislavery activist William Lloyd Garrison, who thundered that the South was trying to make the north "cower and obey like a plantation slave."[19] But reactions such as these served to confirm white southerners' suspicions that the north was out to destroy southern culture and heritage. The two sides, already angry at one another, drifted even further apart after the *Scott* decision.

## Effects

In one sense, the *Dred Scott* decision did not have much impact. Although the Scotts lost their case, Irene Emerson freed them soon afterward. Thus, the verdict had very little effect on them. (Dred Scott died in 1858, having been free for just over a year; Harriet's fate is unclear, but she most likely lived until 1870.) And less than ten years later, following the Civil War, the government not only banned slavery throughout the country but established that native-born blacks were citizens. The decision therefore did not lead to any major policy changes in the way Americans dealt with slavery.

But in another sense, the *Dred Scott* decision had an enormous impact. As much as any other event of its time, it widened the gap between northerners and southerners. As one historian puts it, by showing northerners that their interests were not the same as the interests of southerners, the decision "elected Abraham Lincoln to the presidency."[20] In this way, then, the *Dred Scott* case helped spark the Civil War—and led to the end of slavery. It is paradoxical, yet fitting, that a decision that so limited the rights of blacks would eventually hasten the day when they would all be free.

# Chapter Two

# Plessy v. Ferguson

In the late 1800s state governments throughout the South passed legislation known collectively as "Jim Crow" laws. These laws separated blacks from whites in most areas of public life. Jim Crow laws established separate schools for the races, directed that black and white train passengers sit in separate cars, and forced blacks and whites apart in restaurants, hotels, and many other places. To make matters worse, African American schools, hotels, and train cars were typically old, crumbling, and poorly equipped, while the resources reserved for whites were of much higher quality.

Jim Crow laws were clearly unfair, but blacks lacked the political strength to overturn them. Because they could not out-vote the whites who set up the Jim Crow system, their only recourse was to the courts. In 1892 a New Orleans group challenged the legality of one of Louisiana's Jim Crow laws. This case, known as *Plessy v. Ferguson*, moved slowly through the legal system and resulted in a far-reaching and important decision by the U.S. Supreme Court. Just as *Scott v. Sandford* was the central court case for African Americans in the pre–Civil War era, *Plessy v. Ferguson* would become the central case for blacks in the late 1800s.

## New Amendments

In December 1865, soon after the close of the Civil War, the United States adopted the Thirteenth Amendment to the Constitution. Direct and to the point, the amendment formally eliminated the institution of slavery in the United States and extended the ban to any territories the nation might acquire. "Neither slavery nor involuntary servitude," the amendment reads, ". . . shall exist within the United States, or any place subject to their jurisdiction."[21]

The Thirteenth Amendment, however, only changed the law; it did not change attitudes. Before the Civil War, nearly all white Americans had believed that blacks were inferior to them. This belief was especially widespread in the South, where white leaders and writers had justified slavery in part by describing blacks

Jim Crow laws separated blacks and whites in most areas of public life, including railway stations like the one pictured here in Jackson, Mississippi, which had a waiting room for whites only.

as lazy, mentally slow, and childlike. As South Carolina politician John Calhoun argued in 1854, freedom should be "a reward reserved for the intelligent, the patriotic, the virtuous and the deserving"—that is, whites—"and not a boon [favor] to be bestowed on a people too ignorant, degraded and vicious, to be capable either of appreciating or of enjoying it."[22]

Now, with the end of slavery, these opinions did not change. The war had done nothing to make white southerners stop thinking of blacks as "ignorant, degraded and vicious," as Calhoun put it. Indeed, the war had in many ways increased white southerners' hostility toward African Americans. The 4 million or so newly freed slaves were constant and unhappy reminders of how far the region had fallen. The only southerners who had benefited from the war, it appeared, were black. And blacks' demands for rights seemed to add insult to injury. The southern white, wrote a black observer, "resented the disposition of the black man to claim his franchise [the vote] about in the same spirit in which a man will shoot a dog which has climbed upon the table and will not get down."[23]

Nor did whites appreciate the actions of their slaves during the war. Some slaves stopped working when Northern troops drew near; others abandoned their masters and fled to the safety of Union lines. These behaviors distressed slave owners who believed they had done nothing to deserve such disloyalty. "Our old cook," commented one white woman, "had been the most indulged and well-treated servant imaginable."[24] Yet this cook had chosen to tell the Northern army where to find her mistress's hidden valuables. Some Southern whites were eager to punish local blacks for these acts of unfaithfulness.

## The Black Codes

Shortly after the adoption of the Thirteenth Amendment, most southern states began passing laws aimed at controlling African Americans. These laws were known as the Black Codes. Black Codes in some states prevented African Americans from attending school. Other laws barred African Americans from voting, serving on juries, owning weapons, or making contracts. Some laws restricted certain stores, hotels, and trains to whites only. And most of the laws stated that blacks could not vote.

# Black Codes in Louisiana

The laws below were part of the Black Codes passed by St. Landry Parish, a governmental unit in Louisiana, in 1865. They indicate how severely the Black Codes of the South limited the movement and freedoms of the region's African Americans.

Sec. 1. No negro shall be allowed to pass within the limits of said parish [that is, enter St. Landry] without special permit in writing from his employer.

Sec. 2. Every negro who shall be found absent from the residence of his employer after ten o'clock at night without a written permit from his employer, shall pay a fine of five dollars. . . .

Sec. 3. No negro shall be permitted to rent or keep a house within said parish. . . .

Sec. 5. No public meetings or congregations of negroes shall be allowed within said parish after sunset. . . .

Sec. 7. No Negro who is not in the military service shall be permitted to carry fire-arms, or any kind of weapons, within the parish, without the special written permission of his employers, approved . . . by the nearest and most convenient chief of patrol.

Quoted in Walter Lynwood Fleming, *Documentary History of Reconstruction*. Reprint, Whitefish, MT: Kessinger, pp. 279–80.

These laws angered many northerners and federal officials. Their goal was not just to free the slaves, but to make African Americans full members of society. But southern state governments were doing their best to sabotage this effort by denying blacks any rights at all. Even northerners who had no particular love for blacks found these attempts appalling. "The men of the North will convert the state of Mississippi into a frog pond before they will allow any such laws,"[25] thundered a Chicago newspaper in response to the passage of Black Codes in Mississippi.

In 1866 federal officials responded by proposing a new constitutional amendment. The first section of the amendment specified that blacks had the same rights as whites. "All persons born or naturalized in the United States," the section reads, "are citizens of the United States and of the State wherein they reside."[26] In 1868 the measure was formally adopted, becoming the Fourteenth Amendment to the Constitution.

**The Fourteenth Amendment, which specified that both blacks and whites had the same rights, was added to the Constitution in 1868.**

The Fourteenth Amendment did stop some of the more brazen attempts to limit African American rights. The federal government also sent troops to safeguard the rights of blacks during the next few years, a period of rebuilding the South known as Reconstruction. Reconstruction was a favorable time for the South's African Americans. Some blacks were elected to state government and even to Congress. Others were able to open businesses and schools. The federal government helped limit violence against blacks, too, by punishing those who beat or killed African Americans.

But most southern whites still were unprepared to accept African Americans as equals. And as time went on, northern outrage over the South's inflexibility began to fade. Stationing federal troops in the South cost money. Northerners had issues of their own to focus on. Moreover, it seemed that the conflicts would never stop. "The whole public are tired out with these annual autumnal outbreaks in the South," wrote a government official about a voting rights question in Mississippi during the mid-1870s. "The great majority are now ready to condemn any interference on the part of the government."[27] In 1877 Reconstruction formally came to an end—and with it, direct federal support for the African Americans of the South.

## Jim Crow

With Reconstruction over, southern governments resumed making laws that restricted and demeaned African Americans. The adoption of the Fourteenth Amendment had made this process a bit more difficult, but without active federal oversight, the states were able to act more or less as they pleased. These laws, adopted in some form or other by every southern state in addition to some states in the north, became known as "Jim Crow" laws.

Like the Black Codes before them, the Jim Crow laws were designed to keep blacks and whites apart—and to keep blacks away from access to power and money. Virginia barred blacks from serving on juries. Mississippi made thousands of African Americans ineligible to vote. Towns reserved some or all of their schools for white children only. By the late 1880s, laws such as these were common across the South. Segregation, or the enforced separation of the races, had become a way of life in the former Confederate states.

The spread of Jim Crow laws was met with resignation by most blacks. Despite their gains during Reconstruction, the African Americans of the South still had little power, little education, and little wealth. For generations, the white people of the South had kept African Americans in ignorance and slavery. A dozen or so years of more favorable treatment had helped, but as a group, the former slaves lacked the know-how and the experience to mount a serious challenge to Jim Crow.

## Louisiana's Response

There was one notable exception, however. That was Louisiana. While Louisiana was unquestionably a slave state—indeed, it had been one of the first states to secede after the election of Abraham Lincoln—it had always been different from its fellow southern states in some important ways. Unlike its neighbors, Louisiana's customs had been heavily influenced by French and Spanish traditions. It had the Confederacy's only large city, the cosmopolitan port of New Orleans. And perhaps most important, Louisiana had the Deep South's only substantial population of free blacks.

Free people of color had always been an important part of life in New Orleans. Indeed, before the Civil War the city had achieved a level of racial tolerance unknown elsewhere in the South. Although free blacks were not included in every aspect of the city's development—they were not allowed to vote, for example —they did establish churches, set up schools, and participate in the arts. Many African Americans in New Orleans were well educated, and quite a few were well off by nineteenth-century standards. They were numerous, too. New Orleans was home to more than ten thousand free blacks when the Civil War began.

That history made the African Americans of New Orleans react with particular anger in the late 1880s, when Louisiana considered Jim Crow legislation of its own. Accustomed to a high level of racial tolerance, members of the black community strongly objected to white attempts to limit where they could go and what they could do. But that same history also allowed New Orleans blacks to do something with their anger. The black business leaders, lawyers, and writers of the city spoke out against the proposed laws. They mobilized ordinary African Americans to complain about them, too. Literate, well-off, and aware of their legal rights, New Orleans blacks were able to organize a response in a way that African Americans elsewhere in the South could not.

## The Separate Car Act

For many black people in New Orleans, one of the more objectionable of these proposed new laws had to do with seating in trains. In May 1890 a proposed "Railway Segregation Act" came before the Louisiana state legislature. If passed, this bill would establish "separate but equal"[28] train cars for whites and for blacks. Thus, it would keep blacks and whites apart from each other as they rode on trains within the state.

The proposed law was patterned after similar legislation already passed in other southern states. Legislators in these states had argued that the law was designed to protect African Americans from the hostility of white passengers. Florida's legislation, in fact, specified that "no white person shall be allowed to ride in a negro car or to insult or annoy negroes in such car."[29] Under this new legislation, lawmakers in these states pointed out, blacks would be guaranteed comfortable seating in a racism-free environment.

But most blacks in New Orleans were not convinced. Many objected to the enforced separation of the races under the proposed law. "Such legislation," one protester charged, "is unconstitutional, un-American, unjust [and] dangerous."[30] Others doubted that the accommodations would be truly equal. "In every one of the Gulf states," pointed out a black leader, "the Negro is forced to ride in railroad coaches that are inferior in every way to those given the white."[31] It seemed unlikely that Louisiana would be any different.

Despite intense lobbying by Louisiana's African Americans, though, the state legislature passed the Separate Car Act in July 1890. Riding in the "wrong" car was now a punishable offense, the penalty "a fine of Twenty Five Dollars or . . . imprisonment for a period of not more [than] twenty days."[32] The blacks who had spoken out against the law decided to try to overturn the legislation. But with the state government against them, African American leaders saw only one avenue for satisfaction: the courts.

A black man is ordered from a "whites-only" railway car in nineteenth-century Philadelphia. Legislators passed laws promoting segregation by arguing that the separation of the races would protect black people from racism.

## Homer Plessy

Their strategy was straightforward. Lawyers often use so-called "test cases" to challenge laws they believe to be unconstitutional. In a test case, lawyers and other leaders get a volunteer to break the law in question. When the volunteer is arrested, lawyers file suit on his or her behalf. The black leaders of New Orleans resolved to put together a test case for the Separate Car Act. The only issue was finding the best possible volunteer.

In the end, they chose a man named Homer Plessy to challenge the law. Not yet thirty years old, Plessy was a shoemaker by trade, a lifelong resident of New Orleans, and a member of an African American political organization called the Comité des Citoyens, or Citizens' Committee. Seven of Plessy's eight great-grandparents had been of European origin, but the other had been black. In complexion, Plessy took after his European ancestors. Under Louisiana's complex laws governing race, though, that black ancestor was the only one that counted. Legally, Plessy was black.

# Test Cases and the *Scopes* Trial

*Plessy v. Ferguson* was a test case, in which Homer Plessy, supported by legal and community organizations, deliberately broke the law in order to test its constitutionality. The *Plessy* case is among the most famous test cases in American history, but another of these was the trial of John T. Scopes, a science teacher in Tennessee. In 1925 Tennessee passed a law that barred teachers from introducing the theory of evolution into their classes. Backed by the American Civil Liberties Union, Scopes immediately violated the law by teaching a class from a science text that accepted evolution. The famous attorney Clarence Darrow represented Scopes; former presidential candidate William Jennings Bryan represented the state. Known sometimes as the Tennessee "Monkey Trial," the case ended in a ruling against Scopes, though the verdict was later overturned because of a technicality. Today, however, thanks in part to Darrow's clever questioning of Scopes, the *Scopes v. Tennessee* case is widely remembered as a victory for Scopes and for the teaching of evolution.

On June 7, 1892, Plessy arrived at a train station in New Orleans, bought a ticket, and boarded the car reserved for whites. No one stopped him; no one had any reason to believe that this well-dressed, light-skinned man was not white. But as the train was about to pull out of the station, Plessy spoke to the conductor. "I have to tell you," he said, "that, according to Louisiana law, I am a colored man."[33] Slightly befuddled, the conductor instructed Plessy to move to the car reserved for blacks. When Plessy politely refused, the conductor summoned a police officer, who repeated the conductor's demand. "The law is the law and must be obeyed,"[34] he said. When Plessy still would not vacate his seat, the officer placed him under arrest. The test case was under way.

## The Trial Begins

Plessy's trial began in October 1892. Lawyers for the state introduced evidence that Plessy had violated the Separate Car Act. Plessy's attorneys did not challenge this evidence. Instead, they argued against the law itself. Plessy's skin color made it clear, they noted, that it was difficult, if not impossible, to tell at a glance who was white and who was black. Race was a complicated scientific question, Plessy's lawyers argued, and the Separate Car Act erred by requiring conductors to make these decisions by themselves. It was inappropriate, the lawyers asserted, to "confer upon a conductor the power to determine the question of race."[35]

Plessy's lawyers also argued that the law violated the Constitution. The Fourteenth Amendment, they pointed out, guaranteed the rights of all citizens, blacks included. Plessy's legal team did not see why some citizens but not others should be permitted to ride in a certain train car. In their eyes, the goal of increasing the comfort of both white and black passengers did not justify the infringement of African Americans' constitutional rights. Plessy's lawyers asked the court to throw out the case and to declare the Separate Car Act void.

In November, the judge in the case, a man named John Ferguson, issued his ruling. It was not favorable to Plessy. The state, Ferguson ruled, was entitled to assign seats in train cars if it chose to do so. In Ferguson's opinion, that was a legitimate means of keeping order in society. Thus, Ferguson refused to overrule the law—or overturn Plessy's arrest. Plessy appealed to the Louisiana Supreme Court, but that court upheld Ferguson's decision.

Plessy's lawyers were not dismayed, however. They had expected these results. Their hope, instead, lay in their next move: an appeal to the U.S. Supreme Court.

## More Arguments

The appeal took time. After a number of delays, though, the Supreme Court was finally ready to hear Plessy's case in 1896. Because Plessy was now suing the judge who had refused to rule in his favor, the case was now known as *Plessy v. Ferguson*. Unfortunately for Plessy, the makeup of the court in 1896 was not favorable to him. Nearly all the members of the Court routinely voted against protections for African Americans. The only exception was Justice John Harlan. Though a former slaveholder himself, Harlan had advocated several times for the rights of blacks. Plessy's lawyers hoped that Harlan would not only support Plessy in this case, but convince other justices to take his side as well.

Plessy's attorney, Albion Tourgée, opened the case by repeating his earlier argument that the establishment of separate train cars for the races violated the Fourteenth Amendment. He asked the justices to think about other laws a state might pass if the Separate Car Act was in fact constitutional. What, Tourgée wondered, would prevent a state from making a law that barred redheaded people from riding in a certain car? By making comparisons such as these, Tourgée hoped to hold the law up to ridicule—and to make the point that no group of citizens would be truly safe from discrimination.

Most important, though, Tourgée contended that the law existed for one reason only: to deprive African Americans of their rights. Pointing to the discrimination faced by blacks throughout their history in North America, Tourgée charged that the Separate Car Act was "an attempt to evade the constitutional requirements of equality."[36] That, he argued, was unacceptable and dangerous.

Lawyers for the defense offered arguments of their own. First, they said that Louisiana needed to keep its people safe. If separating the races on railroad cars improved public safety, then the state had a right to do it. Second, they pointed out that the act guaranteed "equal but separate accommodations"[37] for the races. Since the law

Albion Tourgée (pictured) argued for Homer Plessy in the landmark case *Plessy v. Ferguson.*

used the word *equal*, the defense argued, it made little sense to say that the act discriminated against blacks. Third, they noted that segregation was a way of life across the South and much of the north too. And finally, the defense asserted that the matter was a case for the state of Louisiana—not the federal government.

## The Verdict

The verdict was delivered in May 1896. Justice Henry Brown delivered the opinion for the majority—a decision strongly against Plessy. Brown dismissed the idea that accepting the Separate Car Act would necessarily mean that similar laws aimed at other classes of citizens—such as redheads—must be accepted. "Every exercise of the police power must be reasonable," he wrote pointedly, "and not [simply] for the annoyance or oppression of a particular class."[38] And in the opinion of the Court, he continued, separating the races was perfectly reasonable. Not only was segregation a long-standing custom, but keeping whites and blacks apart, in Brown's view, reduced racial violence.

Brown added that Plessy's case was deeply flawed for another reason. The problem, the Court explained, lay in Plessy's "assumption that the enforced separation of the two races stamps the colored race with a badge of inferiority." Brown stated that the new law did no such thing. If African Americans believed that the

Supreme Court justice Henry Brown gave the verdict against Homer Plessy, which upheld legal segregation.

# Harlan's Dissent

Only one Supreme Court justice accepted Homer Plessy's argument. That was John Harlan, whose dissent offered a ringing endorsement of the principles of the United States, as he saw them, and their connection to race:

> Sixty millions of whites are in no danger from the presence here of eight millions of blacks. The destinies of the two races, in this country, are indissolubly linked together, and the interests of both require that the common government of all shall not permit the seeds of race hate to be planted under the sanction of law. What can more certainly arouse race hate, what more certainly create and perpetuate a feeling of distrust between these races, than state enactments [laws], which, in fact, proceed on the ground that colored citizens are so inferior and degraded that they cannot be allowed to sit in public coaches occupied by white citizens? That, as all will admit, is the real meaning of such legislation as was enacted in Louisiana. . . .
>
> If evils will result from the commingling [mixing] of the two races upon public highways established for the benefit of all, they will be infinitely less than those that will surely come from state legislation regulating the enjoyment of civil rights upon the basis of race. We boast of the freedom enjoyed by our people above all other peoples. But it is difficult to reconcile that boast with a state of the law which, practically, puts the brand of servitude and degradation upon a large class of our fellow-citizens, our equals before the law.

> Quoted in Harvey Fireside, *Separate and Unequal.* New York: Carroll and Graf, 2004, pp. 353–54.

**John Harlan was the only Supreme Court justice to accept Homer Plessy's argument.**

Separate Car Act made them inferior, Brown's opinion continued, "it is not by reason of anything found in the act, but solely because the colored race chooses to put that construction upon it"[39]—that is, to interpret it in such a way.

Of the justices on the Court, only Harlan disagreed with Brown's opinion. Though badly outvoted, Harlan nonetheless wrote a stinging dissent in support of Plessy. He accepted the arguments made by Plessy's legal team, notably the notion that the Separate Car Act violated the Fourteenth Amendment by depriving blacks of their rights. To him, racial discrimination made a mockery of the amendment, the Constitution, and American ideals. "Our Constitution is color-blind, and neither knows nor tolerates classes among citizens," he wrote. "In respect of civil rights, all citizens are equal before the law."[40] But stirring as Harlan's words were, they had no effect on his colleagues. The test case had failed. The Court had upheld the Separate Car Act.

## Aftermath

*Plessy v. Ferguson* had an immediate effect across the country. The decision emboldened southern governments—and some in the north as well—that wanted to establish further restrictions on blacks and increase segregation. And despite the emphasis on "equal" accommodations for members of both races, few if any governments, railroad companies, or other organizations offered blacks anything resembling true equality. Phone booths, waiting rooms, schools, theaters—in each case accommodations for blacks were indeed separate, but far from equal.

Over the next fifty years, in fact, the history of African Americans was shaped largely by the Supreme Court's decision in *Plessy v. Ferguson*. Despite Harlan's dissent, the verdict made it clear that all citizens were emphatically *not* equal before the law. The ruling allowed states to treat blacks as second-class citizens at best, and many states, especially in the South, did exactly that. By law, African Americans were kept from voting, relegated to inferior train cars, barred from theaters, and educated in inferior schools. The Court's decision was not by any means the only cause of this legalized bigotry, but it played an important role. As historian Harvey Fireside sums it up, *Plessy v. Ferguson* was the "decision that legalized racism."[41]

## Chapter Three

# Brown v. Board of Education

The African American struggle for civil rights during the 1950s and 1960s ranks as one of the most important events in black history—and in the history of the United States as well. Fed up with segregation and discrimination, African Americans, particularly in the South, began agitating for their civil rights— the rights automatically due to all citizens. Those who took part in the civil rights movement were met with hostility, name-calling, and violence from whites unwilling to change attitudes that had persisted for generations. Indeed, a few civil rights workers were brutally murdered for attempting to bring justice and equality to the African Americans of the South.

Yet the movement was also remarkably successful. Between 1950 and the early 1970s, African Americans made tremendous gains politically, legally, and socially. Bus companies abandoned their segregationist policies. Restaurants that once had served only white customers began to serve African Americans as well. Schools, at least in theory, became open to both blacks and whites. While prejudice and resentment did not disappear, the lives of African Americans became notably better in many important respects.

These gains were made possible by the hard work of thou-sands of dedicated activists, many of whom challenged the system of segregation in dramatic and compelling ways. Alabama activist Rosa Parks, for example, was arrested for refusing to yield her seat on a bus to a white man. Martin Luther King Jr., a Baptist minister, spoke and wrote eloquently about the need for change. Many others risked their lives to vote, to lead protest marches, and to organize their communities. Photographs and video footage of these events—of King's "I Have a Dream" speech, of peaceful protestors being attacked by police dogs, of black students integrating formerly all-white schools—remain well known and powerful today.

But the civil rights movement operated on several different fronts, and not all activists did their work in the high-profile streets and rural areas of the South. Some operated behind the scenes, away from the glare of news cameras and the mobs of angry whites. These activists focused their efforts instead on fighting for change in the legal system. Indeed, the lawyers who worked through the courts achieved some victories critical to the success of the movement— chief among them a triumph in a 1954 Supreme Court case known as *Brown v. Board of Education.*

## Segregation and Schools

During the Jim Crow era in the South, indications of blacks' lower status were everywhere. It was difficult for African Americans to go for long without a reminder of their social and political inferiority. Those who boarded buses and trains found their seating restricted. Those

Although segregation was to provide "separate but equal" facilities for black and white students, black students almost always attended schools vastly inferior to those of their white counterparts, as shown in this segregated Georgia school in 1941.

with jobs saw their white counterparts enjoying better pay and superior working conditions. But no symbol of discrimination was as powerful—or as prevalent—as the public school systems of the South.

Throughout the South and in parts of the north as well, segregation in schools was the law. Technically, the districts that adopted this system provided schools that were not only separate, but equal. But as with the train cars of 1890s Louisiana, the reality was quite different. Schools reserved for white children were newer and in better condition. Teachers at whites-only schools had better training and got higher salaries. And black children were denied services that whites took for granted. "I had to walk to school every day and back no matter if it was storming," recalled one Alabama woman about her childhood. "We could not ride the [school] buses although we were paying taxes. . . . Nothing rode the bus but the whites."[42]

In the 1920s and 1930s, though, most African Americans despaired of changing the system. The precedent set by *Plessy v. Ferguson* was clear: States could do as they pleased where race was concerned. The few legal challenges to enforced segregation in the public schools had gone nowhere. Indeed, black activist W.E.B. DuBois more or less gave up on the notion of trying to abolish segregated schooling. "Negro children [need] neither segregated schools nor mixed schools," he said at one point. "What they need is education."[43]

## Graduate Students Challenge Segregation

The first important legal cases involving segregation in schools, then, did not deal with elementary schools or with high schools. Instead, they dealt with students hoping to pursue graduate studies. The first of these, dating from the 1930s, centered on Donald Murray, a young African American college graduate from Maryland. Murray was eager to become a lawyer, so he applied to the University of Maryland School of Law, a public institution supported by Maryland's taxpayers.

Despite Murray's qualifications, though, the law school refused to accept him. It had never had a black student before, and school officials were not interested in changing that policy. The school offered Murray a very small scholarship to help defray his costs at Howard University, an all-black school in Washington, D.C., but made it clear that he was not welcome to study at Maryland. Murray, however, did not want to go to Howard. With the help of a young black lawyer named Thurgood Marshall and a recently formed organization called the NAACP—the National Association for the Advancement of Colored People—Murray filed suit against the state, alleging that his rights as a citizen had been violated.

Murray's case was heard by a state court. Arguing for Murray, Marshall pointed out that Howard's law school was not in Maryland. By attending Howard, Marshall noted, Murray would not become familiar with Maryland's legal system. Nor would he get to know the judges, prosecutors, and law professors of the state

Thurgood Marshall (left) won the first major court case against segregation when he successfully sued the University of Maryland to force them to admit Donald Murray (center).

who could serve as valuable contacts and sources of information. That would put Murray at a disadvantage when it came to practicing law in Maryland after graduation.

The court agreed with Marshall. Keeping the law school segregated, the court ruled, could cause significant harm to Murray's career. That harm outweighed any interest the school had in keeping blacks away from whites. The university's appeal was likewise dismissed; the next court to hear the case concluded that the school was not following a separate-but-equal policy. "Donald Murray was not sent to a separate school at the University of Maryland," the judges noted. "Donald Murray was excluded from the University of Maryland entirely."[44] The court instructed that Murray be admitted to the school, which he was.

The Murray verdict was followed by a similar decision in the case of another African American student named Lloyd Gaines. Like Murray, Gaines had applied for admission to his state university's law school—in this case, the law school at the University of Missouri—but had been turned down because of his race. As in Maryland, the University of Missouri made no provision for black students, separate or otherwise. Gaines lost his case in the Missouri courts, but appealed to the U.S. Supreme Court, which reversed the Missouri court's ruling. The Gaines case thus extended the precedent begun in *Murray* to the federal level.

## The *Sweatt* Case

More cases followed. Among the most important was the case of *Sweatt v. Painter*, which reached the Supreme Court in 1950. Herman Sweatt was a Texan who was rejected by the University of Texas Law School when he sought admission. Sweatt quickly filed suit. A local court, noting that Texas, like Missouri and Maryland, offered no legal training to African Americans, gave the state a choice: It could either admit blacks or set up a separate law school for them.

Aware of the rulings in the previous cases, Texas chose the latter course. Compared to the already-existing law school at the university, though, the new school was inferior. It had a far smaller library and no reputation to speak of. Nor did it offer students the same opportunities to gain experience in their field. Unsatisfied, Sweatt carried his case to the U.S. Supreme Court.

The Supreme Court issued a ruling in the *Sweatt* case in June 1950. The verdict was unanimous and represented a major victory for the plaintiffs. Judges agreed that Texas's new law school was not comparable to the one already in existence. In prestige, in funding, in the opportunities they offered, the two schools were not remotely equal. "It is difficult to believe," wrote Chief Justice Fred Vinson, "that [a student] who had a free choice between these law schools would consider the question close."[45] Texas's attempt to meet the needs of Sweatt was seriously flawed—and was now invalid.

Black activists were delighted by the outcome in these cases. It was true that the gains had been small. Equality for a handful of ambitious, well-educated students did not mean equality for all African Americans. And the doctrine of separate-but-equal was very far from dead. Thus far, the courts had refused to reconsider *Plessy v. Ferguson* in any of these rulings. Still, the decisions in

After successfully challenging the school's segregation policy, Herman Sweatt sits in his first law class at the University of Texas.

# The *McLaurin* Case

At the same time as it heard *Sweatt v. Painter*, the Supreme Court heard a similar case known as *McLaurin v. Oklahoma State Regents*. This case dealt with George McLaurin, a black teacher from Oklahoma who wanted an advanced degree in education. When the University of Oklahoma told him he was unwelcome, a federal court overruled school administrators and ordered them to admit McLaurin.

Oklahoma accepted the ruling, but grudgingly. University officials forced McLaurin to eat alone in the school dining hall and to study in a separate part of the library. In the classroom, he sat behind a barrier, separated from other students while professors lectured. McLaurin was not happy with this treatment, and he took his dissatisfaction to the Supreme Court.

The justices ruled unanimously in McLaurin's favor. The Court noted that McLaurin's experiences as a student at the University of Oklahoma could not possibly be equal to the experiences of white students at the same institution. The restrictions on McLaurin, the Court ruled, "impair and inhibit his ability to study, to engage in discussions and exchange views with other students, and, in general, to learn his profession." Oklahoma could not force white students to treat McLaurin as an equal, the Court conceded. Still, the state needed to allow McLaurin the opportunity to earn acceptance among his fellow students.

Quoted in Austin Sarat, ed., *Race, Law, and Culture*. New York: Oxford University Press, 1997, p. 58.

George McLaurin was forced to sit apart from white students in this classroom at the University of Oklahoma. McLaurin took his discrimination case to the Supreme Court, which ruled in his favor.

cases such as *Gaines* and *Sweatt* were promising. They seemed to indicate a softening of the long-standing legal support for Jim Crow laws and the doctrine of separate but equal.

## Public Schools Revisited

The verdicts in these cases now emboldened black activists to challenge segregation in the public school systems once more. While the battle would be difficult, it was now possible for leaders like Thurgood Marshall to imagine federal judges striking down laws that kept black and white children apart. In the early 1950s, lawyers for the NAACP found four groups of African American families willing to challenge the segregated school systems in their districts. On behalf of these families, the NAACP filed suit alleging that segregation was causing their children significant harm.

The suits moved forward slowly. Many of the judges who heard these cases were sympathetic to the plaintiffs. But they generally felt constrained to rule according to *Plessy v. Ferguson*, which permitted states to set up separate facilities for blacks and for whites. Accordingly, the initial rulings in three of these cases went against the plaintiffs. The exception was a Delaware case known as *Gebhart v. Belton*, and even this decision affected only the students named in the suit. In these early decisions, in fact, only one judge spoke out loudly against segregation. That was J. Waties Waring, a South Carolina judge whose dissent in a case known as *Briggs v. Elliott* described school segregation as "an evil that must be eradicated."[46]

NAACP leaders were not dismayed by the generally unfavorable rulings. They had expected as much. They appealed each defeat; the state of Delaware, in turn, appealed the ruling in *Gebhart v. Belton*. The NAACP's goal was not just to force the districts to admit the black students to the schools they wanted to attend; in addition, black leaders wanted to overturn the *Plessy* verdict altogether. They hoped to convince the Supreme Court to outlaw segregation in schools—and if possible, in all other aspects of life as well.

## The *Brown* Case

The cases began coming to the Supreme Court in 1952, a time when the civil rights movement had hit its stride. Activists throughout the South were launching full-scale challenges to the concept of separate-but-equal. Race in general, and the issue of segregation in particular, loomed large in the nation's consciousness. Deciding that the cases were of "such imperative public importance as to require . . . immediate settlement in this Court,"[47] Supreme Court officials put the four lawsuits on a faster track— and chose to consider all four at once. The first to be filed was a case called *Brown v. Board of Education of Topeka*, which challenged the segregated elementary schools of Topeka, Kansas. As a result, the cases became collectively known under this title.

When arguments began in 1952, attorneys for the plaintiffs in the lawsuits did not focus on the unfair allocation of resources to all-white and all-black schools. Part of the reason had to do with the circumstances of the original *Brown* case. Oliver Brown, who had sued the Topeka school board, did not allege that his daughter Linda was getting a substandard education at the all-black school she attended; by most accounts, the school provided a solid curriculum and good teachers. Brown's main concern had to do with distance. The all-black elementary school Linda attended was a long way off, making for a time-consuming and difficult journey each day, but the district would not permit her to enroll in a nearby school reserved for whites only.

More to the point, though, Thurgood Marshall and other civil rights leaders were no longer willing to accept any form of segregation whatever. Several states had fought lawsuits by promising to build newer schools for blacks or by reworking the way districts spent money. Lower court decisions had indicated that many judges might find these measures acceptable. "The court should not use its power to abolish segregation," wrote a South Carolina justice in *Briggs v. Elliott*, "if the equality demanded by the Constitution can be attained otherwise."[48]

A generation or two earlier, leaders like W.E.B. DuBois would have happily agreed to keep segregation if the education offered to blacks were truly equal. Now, though, thinking had changed. Many African American leaders of the 1950s believed that segregation itself was damaging to black children. The separate-but-equal laws were designed to emphasize the inferiority of African Americans, these leaders charged. Black children would feel inferior as long as the system continued. True integration, then, was the only answer.

The plaintiffs in the Supreme Court case *Brown v. Board of Education* are shown here. The case challenged school segregation laws.

## Arguments and Counterarguments

Accordingly, the lawyers' arguments relied heavily on the testimony of psychologists. Kenneth Clark, a researcher who studied some of the children at the center of the court cases, was one of several experts who testified. In Clark's view, black children in segregated schools did indeed feel bad about themselves. "Like other human beings who are subjected to an obviously inferior status in the society in which they live," Clark told judges in the early stages of *Briggs v. Elliott*, black children in segregated South Carolina schools "have been definitely harmed in the development of their personalities."[49]

The NAACP lawyers offered other arguments, too. They noted the Court's recent rulings that supposedly "equal" accommodations

As a witness in the *Brown* case, psychologist Kenneth Clark testified to the psychological harm inflicted on black children as a result of segregation.

for graduate students were not truly equal, and asked the justices to extend this reasoning to schoolchildren as well. They cited scientific research showing that blacks were intellectually the equals of whites, proving that segregation was not based on any rational standard. And they pointed out that black and white children had plenty of contact outside of school. "They play in the streets together," said Marshall, "they play on their farms together, they go down the road together, they separate to go to school, they come out of school and play ball together."[50] Why, he asked, was togetherness acceptable everywhere except school?

Lawyers for the defense had arguments of their own. They emphasized that segregation was based on strong cultural and social values. They questioned the findings of Kenneth Clark and other experts. And as Marshall had predicted, they also pointed to the steps segregated school districts were taking to narrow the gap in resources between whites and blacks. The future for black students, defense lawyers argued, was bright.

The lawyers for the school districts also asserted that the Fourteenth Amendment did not apply to school desegregation cases. Though the amendment barred states from "deny[ing] any person . . . the equal protection of the law,"[51] the school systems argued that the amendment was not as simple as it appeared. In their view, it applied only to the rights listed in an 1866 federal civil rights law which had been passed at the same time as the amendment. That law said nothing about public education. Thus, the lawyers said, the Fourteenth Amendment did not apply to *Brown*.

## A Ruling

At first, the justices seemed hopelessly split. But Chief Justice Earl Warren, a strong proponent of integration, worked tirelessly to change his colleagues' minds. Warren believed that the law was on the side of the NAACP, and he also believed that whites were not as racist as they had been years earlier. Legally and politically, then, Warren was convinced that the time had come to end segregation. One by one, the other justices came around to his way of thinking.

Supreme Court chief justice Earl Warren was instrumental in the Court's rendering a verdict in *Brown v. Board of Education* that effectively ended legal support of segregation in schools.

On May 17, 1954, the Court ruled unanimously in favor of Brown and the other plaintiffs. "In the field of public education," Warren wrote, "the doctrine of 'separate but equal' has no place."[52]

Warren's opinion laid out a clear case against segregation. The Court accepted the plaintiffs' argument that the practice caused psychological harm to black children. Segregation, Warren wrote, "generates a feeling of inferiority [in African Americans] that may affect their hearts and minds in a way unlikely ever to be undone."[53] The justices also ruled that the Fourteenth Amendment did indeed apply to the case. At the time the amendment was written, Warren noted, there were scarcely any public schools. The writers of the amendment probably did not mean to exclude education; they simply did not predict that in less than a century public schools would become, as Warren put it, "perhaps the most important function of state and local government."[54] It

## Excerpt from the *Brown* Decision

In the early stages of the *Brown* case, a Kansas court ruled that *Plessy v. Ferguson* allowed states to segregate schools. However, the judges on the court were uncomfortable with the effects of segregation on black children denied the right to go to the same schools as whites. This excerpt from the Kansas court's ruling was quoted by Earl Warren in his majority opinion for the U.S. Supreme Court in the *Brown* decision of 1954.

Segregation of white and colored children in public schools has a detrimental effect upon the colored children. The impact is greater when it has the sanction of the law, for the policy of separating the races is usually interpreted as denoting the inferiority of the negro group. A sense of inferiority affects the motivation of a child to learn. Segregation with the sanction of law, therefore, has a tendency to [retard] the educational and mental development of negro children and to deprive them of some of the benefits they would receive in a racial[ly] integrated school system.

Quoted in Maureen Harrison and Steve Gilbert, *Great Decisions of the U.S. Supreme Court*. New York: Excellent Books, 2003, p. 79.

was unreasonable, then, to use the specifics of an 1866 law to form public policy nearly a century later. The conclusion, the Court ruled, was that segregated schools violated the equal protection clause of the amendment.

The one remaining question had to do with a timetable. How quickly would school systems be forced to integrate? The Court had plenty of options. The justices could order that all schools be integrated more or less immediately—a position taken by NAACP lawyers—or they could do as the other side requested and allow states and school systems to take small steps toward a distant goal of complete integration. Uncertain how to proceed, the justices issued their ruling without addressing this question. They indicated that they would take this issue up again later on. In the meantime, they were curious to know how Americans—and white southerners in particular—would perceive the decision.

## *Brown II*

The reaction, in fact, was mixed. Many white leaders in the upper South expressed a willingness to abide by the Court's decision. In parts of states like Maryland, Missouri, and Kentucky, a number of districts began desegregating voluntarily. But whites in other areas were much less accepting. Some politicians said that their states might abandon public education altogether if the Court required immediate integration. The Virginia state legislature voted to withdraw state funding from any school that admitted both blacks and whites. And some whites, especially in the Deep South, warned that attempts to enforce the new law might be met with violence.

After much discussion and further arguments by lawyers for both sides, the Supreme Court reached an agreement. States were to "make a prompt and reasonable start toward full compliance" with the decision, the Court wrote in a ruling known as *Brown II*. Rather than specify a deadline, however, the Court simply ordered the states to move ahead "with all deliberate speed."[55] The words were vague, and intentionally so. The justices hoped that each side would be content: African Americans because the ruling insisted on integration, whites because the ruling allowed time for all-white school systems to comply.

But *Brown II* was more controversial than the justices expected. While some blacks complained that the decision did not go

A billboard calls for the impeachment of Supreme Court chief justice Earl Warren in reaction to the Court's ruling against segregation in schools.

nearly far enough in guaranteeing the rights of African Americans, the bigger issue was that the justices underestimated the hostility toward integration among southern whites. Many school systems and state governments refused to accept any timetable at all. Angry mobs formed in some towns and cities to prevent black students from entering previously all-white schools. Politicians won votes by denouncing school desegregation in general and the *Brown* decision in particular. "We're not going to pay any attention to the Supreme Court decision," said Mississippi's governor soon after the decision was announced. "We don't think it will have any effect on us down here at all."[56]

In the short term, at least, he was right. In the years immediately after *Brown II*, very few southern communities made any real progress toward desegregating their schools. Political and educational leaders used legal tricks, empty promises, and threats of violence to avoid integration. In some parts of the region, whites simply abandoned the public school systems for so-called "segregation academies," privately run schools closed to African

American students. By one estimate, a decade after the *Brown* decision was handed down, about 99 percent of southern black children were still attending segregated schools.

The situation did not begin to improve until 1964, the first full year of Lyndon Johnson's presidency. Though a southerner, Johnson was a strong supporter of civil rights legislation and an opponent of segregation in schools. Unlike his predecessors, who had moved relatively slowly where school integration was concerned, Johnson made full use of the power of his office to force states to integrate more quickly. Further lawsuits by attorneys from the NAACP and other civil rights groups helped force some districts and states to desegregate as well. By the mid-1970s, about half of the South's black children were enrolled at integrated schools.

The promise of the *Brown* decision remains elusive. America is not yet a color-blind society. While public school systems throughout the country are open to children of all races, it can be

## Violence in Little Rock

◼

Desegregation of schools did not proceed as smoothly as the Supreme Court had hoped. While some cities and towns integrated peacefully enough, others resisted. One of these cities was Little Rock, Arkansas. In 1957, three years after the original *Brown* ruling, nine black high school students in Little Rock enrolled in Central High School, a formerly all-white institution. They met with angry, violent mobs. As one of the students, Melba Pattillo, recalled afterward:

> The first day I was able to enter Central High School, what I felt inside was terrible, wrenching, awful fear. On the car radio I could hear that there was a mob. I knew what a mob meant and I knew that the sounds that came from the crowd were very angry. So we entered . . . the building very, very fast. Even as we entered there were people running after us. . . . We were met by school officials and very quickly dispersed our separate ways. There has never been in my life any stark terror or any fear akin to that.

Quoted in Henry Hampton and Steve Fayer, *Voices of Freedom*. New York: Bantam, 1990, p. 45.

hard to find schools that mix black and white students as the Supreme Court justices envisioned. But the impact of the *Brown* decision is nonetheless evident. Racial segregation implied full rights for some—and limited rights for others. As Thurgood Marshall said in his argument to the justices, "This Court should make it clear that this is not what our Constitution stands for."[57] By removing the legal basis for segregation in the schools, the *Brown* decision at last extended the full protection of the laws to African Americans.

## Chapter Four

# Voting Rights and Political Power

The civil rights movement was deeply concerned with ending segregation. But it had other goals as well. Civil rights leaders hoped to expand economic opportunities for blacks, for example, by increasing their wages and helping them find higher-paying jobs. They worked to give African Americans a sense of pride in their heritage and an awareness of the achievements of others of their race. And perhaps most important of all, civil rights activists were eager to expand the voting rights of African Americans.

In theory, American blacks of the 1950s and early 1960s had the right to vote. The reality, however, was usually quite different. State and local governments across the South—and sometimes beyond—did everything in their power to deny most African Americans the chance to cast a ballot. Civil rights leaders responded to these efforts with some of the same strategies that had helped them end enforced segregation. Among these strategies was a reliance on the courts. That reliance paid off; some of the civil rights movement's biggest gains were the result of court decisions.

Compared to decisions such as *Dred Scott* and *Brown v. Board of Education*, the voting rights cases of the 1950s and 1960s are

# Blacks and Voting Rights

―――――――――――◼――――――――――――

Some free blacks were allowed to vote in the years before the Civil War. Their right to cast a ballot, however, depended very much on the particular circumstances of their time and place. In the years immediately following the American Revolution, for example, African Americans could vote in New York, New Hampshire, and several other states. Even North Carolina, a staunch slaveholding state, permitted free blacks to vote during the late 1700s and the early 1800s.

However, these rights were shaky, and many were modified or eliminated altogether as time passed. North Carolina, for example, revoked the right of African Americans to vote in 1835. The situation was not much different in the North. "By 1840," writes historian Derrick Bell, "93 percent of the northern free black population lived in states that completely or practically excluded them from the right to vote." At the time of the Civil War, then, only a tiny fraction of the nation's more than 4 million African Americans were legally entitled to cast a ballot.

Derrick Bell, *Silent Covenants*. New York: Oxford University Press, 2004, p. 34.

not well known today. No voting rights case is studied in modern times as history students study *Plessy* or *Brown*; no voting rights case resulted in a ruling as sweeping as the *Dred Scott* decision. Still, the relative obscurity of voting rights cases does not imply that they were unimportant. By bringing African Americans into the political arena, these cases allowed blacks to participate in society in a way that had once been impossible.

## The Right to Vote

Throughout American history, voting rights for blacks have been sharply curtailed much more often than not. The roots of this policy lay in slavery. Keeping slaves from voting was certainly in the interest of slave-owning southerners, especially in areas where African American slaves far outnumbered whites. Legally speaking, moreover, slaves were not citizens. Therefore they did not share most of the rights enjoyed by free Americans, among them the right to cast a ballot.

But even free blacks in early America were often denied the vote. For years, virtually all whites believed that people of African heritage were inferior to those whose ancestors came from Europe. Intellectually and morally, the argument ran, blacks were less fully developed than whites. African Americans, even those who were not enslaved, could not properly exercise the responsibility of casting a ballot. Even northern whites who were highly sympathetic to blacks were not always willing to offer them voting rights. "Though it is not their fault that they have been kept brutally ignorant," wrote antislavery activist Lydia Maria Child in 1839, "it unfits them for voters."[58]

The Reconstruction era that followed the Civil War, however, ushered in an enormous change. The Fourteenth Amendment, approved in 1868, guaranteed civil rights for African Americans and established that blacks could be U.S. citizens. When several southern states attempted to pass laws limiting the right of black

During the era of Reconstruction following the Civil War, African Americans had the protection of the federal government to ensure their right to vote.

men to vote, the federal government responded by drafting the Fifteenth Amendment. This amendment, ratified in 1870, specifically addresses voting rights. As Section 1 puts it, "The right of citizens of the United States to vote shall not be denied or abridged by the United States or by any State on account of race, color, or previous condition of servitude."[59]

The law was clear, then. And its results were heartening. Despite widespread illiteracy and threats from white racists, blacks turned out to vote in large numbers. In the early 1870s, nearly half the voters in Louisiana were African American. But when Reconstruction came to an end, the voting rights of black southerners became vulnerable once more. Without the presence of federal troops, new laws and customs increasingly kept blacks from casting ballots. By 1898 fewer than one Louisiana voter in twenty was black. And that number was high in comparison to the figures for many other southern states.

## Intimidation, Taxes, and Literacy

In the decades following Reconstruction, white politicians used several methods to lower voter turnout among African Americans while adhering to the letter of the Fifteenth Amendment. One of the most common was intimidation. Whites frequently threatened to retaliate against blacks who dared to vote—or even to register as prospective voters. African Americans who ignored the warnings were savagely beaten. Their houses were burned to the ground. Many were fired from their jobs.

This campaign of violence was quite successful in most places. While most blacks were eager to vote, few were willing to risk the consequences. And the only law enforcement officials in most areas were squarely on the side of the intimidators. The 1955 case of George Lee, a black minister from Belzoni, Mississippi, illustrates both the level of brutality and the involvement of local police in the violence. That spring, Lee registered to vote, making him the only African American voter in his heavily black county. Soon afterward, as one history of the civil rights movement puts it, Lee "was killed by a shotgun blast to the face. Local authorities ruled his death a traffic accident."[60]

A more subtle ploy to keep blacks from voting was the use of a so-called poll tax. A poll tax was a fee that voters were required

Hostile whites attempted to prevent blacks from voting through violence and intimidation.

to pay before they were allowed to cast their ballots. By modern standards, the charges were not high—in Mississippi during the early 1960s, the tax was $2—but for the time and place, the fee was generally more than most African Americans could afford. By establishing a sufficiently high poll tax, then, state governments could keep most blacks from voting. And in the years following Reconstruction, governments did exactly that. According to some estimates, poll taxes alone prevented more than 90 percent of African Americans from voting in many areas of the South.

A similar tactic involved literacy. Virtually all slaves were unable to read; in many slave states, in fact, teaching a slave to read was against the law. In the years immediately after the Civil War, teachers set up schools designed to teach the fundamentals of reading to black children and adults. One of these teachers, an African American named Susie Baker King Taylor, was deeply touched by the former slaves she taught, grown men and women "so eager to learn to read, to read above anything else."[61] Many of these African Americans did indeed become quite literate. And of course some free blacks, particularly in New Orleans, were as well educated as any white southerner.

But segregated schools, the long hours most blacks needed to work in order to put food on the table, and the legacy of slavery combined to make literacy relatively rare among southern blacks of the period, and state and local governments took full advantage of this fact. Many governments approved legislation requiring that citizens pass a literacy test before being allowed to cast their ballots. Knowing that they could never pass such a test, however easy, thousands of African Americans did not even attempt to vote. Like the poll taxes, literacy exams kept many African Americans from participating in government.

## Grandfather Clauses and More

Poll taxes and literacy requirements were effective in keeping black turnout down at the polls. At the same time, however, they threatened to disqualify many white voters as well. The South had plenty of whites who scrabbled out a bare living on farms and could not afford poll taxes. Many of these people, moreover, were no more literate than the former slaves. But white political leaders did not want to prevent poor, illiterate whites from voting.

Southern states used two strategies to keep blacks from voting while allowing whites to cast their ballots. One was known as the grandfather clause. Grandfather clauses stated that poll taxes or literacy requirements did not apply to all voters. If a man's father or grandfather had been a legal voter by the rules of an earlier time, usually at the close of the Civil War, then the man was exempt from paying the tax or passing the literacy test. He would be eligible to cast a ballot regardless of his financial situation or his ability to read and write.

These clauses were designed to make sure that nearly all white voters in the South were qualified to vote. Their fathers and grandfathers, however poor or illiterate, had been able to vote simply by virtue of being white. Immigrants were typically "grandfathered in" by these clauses as well. As Oklahoma's grandfather clause put it, "no person who . . . resided in some foreign nation, and no lineal descendant of such person[,] shall be denied the right to vote"[62] because of illiteracy. At the same time, the fathers and grandfathers of practically all African Americans in the South had been enslaved and ineligible to vote. Only blacks, then, were required to pay poll taxes and pass literacy tests.

Whites attempted to prevent blacks from voting by forcing them to take literacy tests before they could vote. Poll workers could make these tests too difficult for most African Americans to pass.

### EXCERPTS FROM THE CONSTITUTION

Part 1. In case of the removal of the president from office, or of his death, resignation, or inability to discharge the powers and duties of the said office, the same shall devolve on the vice-president, and the congress may by law provide for the case of removal, death, resignaton or inability, both of the president and vice-president, declaring what officer shall then act as president, and such officer shall act accordingly, until the disability be removed, or a president shall be elected.

Part 2. In all cases affecting ambassadors, other public ministers and consuls, and those in which a state shall be a party, the supreme court shall have original jurisdiction.

Part 3. In all the other cases before mentioned, the supreme court shall have appellate jurisdiction, both as to law and fact, with such exceptions, and under such regulations as the congress shall make.

Part 4. Neither slavery nor involuntary servitude, except as a punishment for crime whereof the party shall have been duly convicted, shall exist within the United States, or any place subject to their jurisdiction.

---

### INSTRUCTION "C"

(After applicant has read, not aloud, the foregoing excerpts from the Constitution, he will answer the following questions in writing and without assistance:)

---

1. In case the president is unable to perform the duties of his office, who assumes them? _____

2. "Involuntary servitude" is permitted in the United States upon conviction of a crime. (True or False)_____

3. If a state is a party to a case, the constitution provides that original jurisdiction shall be in_____

4. Congress passes laws regulating cases which are included in those over which the United States Supreme Court has_____

_____ jurisdiction.

---

I hereby certify that I have received no assistance in the completion of this citizenship and literacy test, that I was allowed the time I desired to complete it, and that I waive any right existing to demand a copy of same. (If for any reason the applicant does not wish to sign this, he must discuss the matter with the board of registrars.)

Signed: _____
(Applicant)

Another way to allow poor and illiterate whites to vote without extending the same privileges to African Americans was to apply different standards to whites and blacks who tried to register. In Alabama, for example, applicants in the 1950s were required to read a section of the Constitution. Which section was up to the registrar, the government official in charge of registering voters. "The registrar could assign you a long complex section filled with legalese and convoluted sentences," one observer reports, "or he could tell you to read a simple one or two sentence section."[63] The more complicated sections were invariably given to African Americans; the easier sections were assigned to whites.

Even reading the material correctly and effectively did not guarantee that a candidate would be allowed to vote. It was the registrar's responsibility to determine whether an applicant passed or failed, and race played an enormous role in the decision. In Mississippi, one would-be registrant recalled, "One of the questions was, Interpret any of the two hundred eighty-six sections of the Mississippi constitution to the satisfaction of the registrar. . . . Some of these registrars couldn't read or write, but that didn't matter; they could still determine who should be registered."[64] All through the South, registrars arbitrarily failed African Americans who took literacy tests, thus keeping them from casting a vote.

## Early Challenges

These laws violated the spirit, if not the letter, of the Fifteenth Amendment. In the early 1900s several attorneys sued states on behalf of blacks who were being denied the right to vote. The courts typically sided with the states. In the 1937 case of *Breedlove v. Suttles,* for instance, the Supreme Court upheld the use of poll taxes. To be sure, federal judges sometimes did declare that certain laws were unconstitutional attempts to defy the Fifteenth Amendment. But even when judges ruled in favor of the plaintiffs, little changed. States and counties simply resorted to more subtle methods of keeping African Americans from voting.

The 1915 case of *Guinn v. United States* was an excellent example. In this decision, the Supreme Court struck down the grandfather clauses adopted by several states, most notably Oklahoma.

Oklahoma's grandfather clause, the justices conceded, contained "no express words" that referred to "race, color, or previous condition of servitude,"[65] and so by that standard was not in violation of the Fifteenth Amendment. However, the justices continued, the law had clearly been drawn up to exclude African Americans, which was unacceptable.

Oklahoma did not change its ways, however. It simply passed a new law. According to this law, all people who had registered before 1914 remained eligible to vote. That encompassed nearly all the states' whites. Blacks of voting age were given a twelve-day period in which to register. Those who did not register in this time frame would be forever ineligible to vote. The new law had the effect of sharply limiting black voting, just as the old law had done. The new law remained on the books in Oklahoma until 1939, when the Supreme Court finally declared it a violation of the Fifteenth Amendment as well.

The truth was that changing the system through legal maneuvering was extremely difficult. Supreme Court justice Oliver Wendell Holmes explained the dilemma in his opinion for *Giles v. Harris*, a 1903 voting rights case from Alabama. Holmes pointed out that the Court could tell states and county election boards what to do, but could not easily enforce its instructions. According to the *Giles* case, he noted, "the great mass of [Alabama's] white population intends to keep the blacks from voting. To [fight back against] such an intent something more than ordering the plaintiff's name to be inscribed upon the [registration] lists of 1902 will be needed."[66] Holmes concluded that the responsibility for safeguarding voting rights lay not with the courts, but with Congress.

Still, with Congress uninterested in promoting the rights of blacks, the court system seemed the only real path to change during the first half of the 1900s. Despite the long odds against them, African American activists continued to file suits against those who denied them the vote. And there were occasional victories. In the 1927 case of *Nixon v. Herndon*, for example, the Supreme Court reviewed a law stating that no African American was "eligible to participate in a Democratic party primary election in the State of Texas."[67] In Texas, nearly all voters were Democrats, so the primary election, in which party members picked their candidates, was more important than the general election. Not only did the Court strike down the law, but it also overruled two attempts by Texas to revise the law so it still banned blacks. Lawyers for organizations such as the NAACP appreciated the support of the court system, and dreamed of the day that the Court's decisions could be enforced.

## The Civil Rights Movement

That day drew closer with the beginning of the civil rights movement. One of the most significant cases civil rights attorneys brought to the Supreme Court during this period was a 1960 case called *Gomillion v. Lightfoot*. This case dealt with the small city of Tuskegee, Alabama. Along with most other southern cities, Tuskegee

# The *Gomillion* Case

The excerpt below comes from the Supreme Court's decision in *Gomillion v. Lightfoot*, decided in 1960. In this passage the majority opinion draws a distinction between causing inadvertent harm to blacks while working toward a greater good, and setting out to deliberately go against the interest of African Americans. In this case, the Court ruled, the Alabama legislature had done the latter.

According to the allegations here made, the Alabama Legislature has not merely redrawn the Tuskegee city limits with incidental inconvenience to the petitioners; it is more accurate to say that it has deprived the petitioners [plaintiffs] of the municipal franchise [the ability to vote as a citizen of Tuskegee] and consequent rights and to that end it has incidentally changed the city's boundaries. While in form this is merely an act redefining metes and bounds [borderlines], if the allegations are established, the inescapable human effect of this essay in geometry and geography is to despoil colored citizens, and only colored citizens, of their theretofore enjoyed voting rights.

Blackpast.org, "*Gomillion v. Lightfoot, Mayor of Tuskegee.*" www.blackpast.org/?q=primary/gomillion-v-lightfoot-mayor-tuskegee.

had been governed for years by a group of whites eager to keep African Americans from becoming part of the system.

An increasing number of Tuskegee's African Americans, however, began registering to vote during the late 1950s. White political leaders at the state and local levels worried about the possible impact of all these new voters on the city and its government. Their response was to redraw the city boundary, a process known as gerrymandering. The once-square city became a "strangely irregular twenty-eight-sided figure,"[68] as official documents put it. The new border was by no means random. It placed nearly every black in Tuskegee outside the city limits, while not affecting a single white voter.

Blacks immediately filed suit. By redrawing its city limits, attorneys argued, Tuskegee was trying to keep African Americans out of the political process. The justices of the Supreme Court unanimously agreed. They noted that while Alabama could redraw its election districts, it could not do so as a ploy to limit blacks' voting rights. "Acts generally lawful may become unlawful when done to accomplish an unlawful end,"[69] wrote Justice Felix Frankfurter. In this case, Alabama was guilty of violating the spirit of the Fifteenth Amendment. Tuskegee's boundaries had to remain as they were.

The 1966 case of *Harper v. Virginia Board of Elections* was another important case of this period. Two years earlier, the Twenty-fourth Amendment had gone into effect. This amendment, introduced in 1962, barred states from using poll taxes in federal elections. "There can be no one too poor to vote,"[70] declared President Lyndon Johnson, a strong supporter of voting rights, after the amendment was formally approved. Johnson was not quite right, however. The amendment said nothing about the legality of poll taxes in elections for state offices, and a handful of states—including Virginia—continued to impose them on would-be voters.

Emboldened by the new amendment and the increasing successes of the civil rights movement, though, a poor black woman named Annie Harper sued Virginia to overturn the law that allowed poll taxes. A lower court, feeling bound by the Supreme Court's earlier ruling in *Breedlove v. Suttles*—the 1937 case which had found that poll taxes were constitutional—declined to rule in

Alabama state senator Samuel Engelhardt (pictured) and other officials rezoned the Tuskegee city limits in an effort to deny African Americans their right to vote.

# Demanding the Vote

African Americans used the court system quite effectively in their struggle to earn voting rights. But their best weapon was probably not the lawsuit. Instead, it was the African American people of the South, who courageously demanded their rights after years of being oppressed—and in the face of threats and intimidation from the white majority who ruled the region.

During the civil rights era, activists went door-to-door throughout the South, sometimes under cover of darkness to avoid attracting the attention of hostile whites. They explained the benefits of voting to African Americans who had never considered trying to register. While some were not ready to take this step, others were eager to become involved and to hear the message of these activists. "You can help yourself by trying to register to vote," one Mississippi woman remembers a black civil rights worker telling her in the early 1960s. "That's the first time in my life that I ever come into contact with anybody that tells me that I had the right to register to vote."

Quoted in Henry Hampton and Steve Fayer, *Voices of Freedom*. New York: Bantam, 1990, p. 180.

Harper's favor. But when Harper appealed the decision, the Supreme Court gave her the satisfaction she sought. "Voter qualifications have no relation to wealth," the justices noted in a 6–3 decision for the plaintiff, "nor to paying or not paying this or any other tax."[71] The poll tax was officially dead.

## The Voting Rights Act

Back in 1903 Justice Oliver Wendell Holmes had theorized that Congress, not the courts, would have to secure the voting rights of African Americans. As the events of the 1960s proved, Holmes was correct. The approval of the Twenty-fourth Amendment was one piece of the puzzle. The passage of the Civil Rights Act in 1964 was another; this bill wrote some safeguards to black voting rights into federal law. But the most important of these bills was the Voting Rights Act of 1965.

The Voting Rights Act began with a powerful declaration. "No voting qualification or prerequisite to voting," it read, "or standard, practice, or procedure shall be imposed or applied by any State or political subdivision to deny or abridge the right of any citizen of the United States to vote on account of race or color."[72] The Voting Rights Act thus banned literacy exams along with any other "test or device"[73] that states had used to lower black turnout at the polls. Perhaps more important, it let the federal government oversee elections in states with a history of discriminating against African Americans. Together, the law and the prospect of enforcement raised the hopes of black leaders. It seemed that the voting rights of blacks would finally be guaranteed.

The story was not quite over, however. Leaders of several southern states disagreed with the provisions of the Voting Rights Act. They argued that Congress had gone too far in regulating the

John Doar, Nicholas Katzenbach, and Thurgood Marshall (left to right) successfully defended the Voting Rights Act before the U.S. Supreme Court.

affairs of their states. In 1966 the Supreme Court heard a direct challenge to the Voting Rights Act in a case known as *South Carolina v. Katzenbach*. Although the decision was not unanimous, the justices ruled that Congress was acting reasonably by singling out South Carolina and other states. "Congress had reliable evidence of voting discrimination in a great majority of the[se] areas,"[74] wrote Chief Justice Earl Warren for the majority. And Congress, Warren noted, had the authority to enforce the Fifteenth Amendment. The Voting Rights Act, then, was absolutely acceptable.

## Today

The issue of voting rights for African Americans remains controversial. Some observers argue that it is no longer necessary for Congress to oversee elections to make sure blacks are included. The days of racial discrimination at the polls are over, these people say, and the restrictions placed on state and local governments by the Voting Rights Act are excessive. Other observers, however, assert that governments still make it hard for blacks to vote. In an effort to combat voting fraud, for instance, Indiana recently required voters to produce identification. Opponents of the measure say it will depress turnout among African Americans, especially those who are poor, because they may find it difficult to obtain the proper identification documents.

Still, no one denies that voting rights for African Americans are far better protected than they were before the 1960s. The court system was integral to the change. In early cases such as *Guinn v. United States* and *Nixon v. Herndon*, Supreme Court justices upheld the spirit of the Fifteenth Amendment when no other governing body would do so. In later cases such as *Gomillion v. Lightfoot* and *Harper v. Virginia Board of Elections*, the courts continued to help African American activists chip away at the system that kept so many of them from voting. And in *South Carolina v. Katzenbach*, the courts supported Congress in the government's new willingness to ensure that blacks could vote. Without the rulings of the courts, the road to full voting rights for black Americans would have been much more difficult.

## Chapter Five

# Affirmative Action

One of the thorniest issues in public policy today has to do with affirmative action, or the practice of giving African Americans and members of other minority groups preferential treatment in jobs, college admissions, and other areas of society. Affirmative action has been in use since the 1960s as a way of redressing earlier inequities against blacks. Yet affirmative action has often been deeply controversial, with those in favor and those against bringing strong feelings to the discussion. Even after several decades of debate, Americans have not yet reached a consensus on the question of whether affirmative action is a worthy goal—or, if it is, how it should be implemented.

That has been true not only of Americans in general; it has also been true of the U.S. judicial system. As with slavery, voting rights, and school desegregation, much of the debate over affirmative action has played out in the courts. Over the years, courts have heard dozens of cases that seek to establish the limits of affirmative action. But the rulings of these courts have been inconsistent. Cases that seem similar on the surface are often decided in very different ways by different courts, and unanimous decisions are rare. The debate about affirmative action is still very much alive—and the courts remain a significant part of that debate.

## Early History

The earliest examples of affirmative action did not deal specifically with African Americans, but attempted to level the playing field for members of other groups instead. In the years immediately following World War II, for instance, many colleges offered special treatment to former soldiers. The University of Wisconsin, for example, announced a change in its policies in 1945 "so that veterans of World War II who do not possess all the [standard] requirements for admission may be admitted," as long as they could provide "evidence that they are prepared to take advantageously the subjects open to them."[75] University officials found it

# Affirmative Action: Pro and Con

Those who support affirmative action and those who oppose it generally agree that blacks have been oppressed in the past and that African Americans have still not reached equality with whites in most areas of modern life. Where the two sides diverge is not in their acceptance of these facts, but in their interpretation of them.

Proponents of affirmative action argue that African Americans need extra assistance to move toward equality. They see the problems of blacks today as largely a consequence of generations of mistreatment, and they believe that racism is not yet a thing of the past. To them, it is moral and fair to give modern-day blacks an advantage in being admitted to colleges or hired for municipal jobs. They also argue that increasing diversity is an important goal in an increasingly diverse nation. In their view, it is not in anyone's best interest to have police departments with nothing but white officers or law schools with scarcely any minority students.

Opponents of affirmative action take a different view. To them, affirmative action is simply another form of bias. Since most Americans agree that discrimination is a bad thing, they point out, it makes no sense to fight one kind of racial bias by instituting another kind. They are also troubled by the impact that affirmative action has on whites who seek college admission or a firefighter job. Affirmative action, by its very nature, requires that some well-qualified whites be turned down in favor of blacks whose qualifications are, at least in theory, not as strong.

perfectly appropriate to change the rules for the benefit of one group they considered deserving, while keeping policies the same for everyone else.

Affirmative action for the benefit of blacks is generally considered to have begun in the mid-1960s. The political leader most responsible for promoting and instituting affirmative action was Lyndon Johnson, who served as president from the end of 1963 through early 1969. Johnson was well aware that many employers discriminated against blacks. He believed, however, that simply ending racial biases in hiring practices would not fix the problem. More, Johnson argued, was necessary. As he said in a 1965 speech, "You do not take a person who, for years, has been hobbled by chains and liberate him, bring him up to the starting line of a race and then say, 'You are free to compete with all the others,' and still justly believe that you have been completely fair."[76] To be truly fair, Johnson contended, those who had been "hobbled by chains" needed—and deserved—extra help.

Later in 1965 Johnson acted on his principles by issuing a special directive. This order echoed one written several years earlier by the previous president, John Kennedy; but unlike Kennedy's, which was not well enforced, Johnson intended to make sure his order was followed. Johnson instructed the government "to promote the full realization of equal employment opportunity through a positive, continuing program in each department and agency."[77] With this directive, Johnson was calling for a good deal more than a commitment to hire blacks as well as whites. He was mandating that various federal offices make a concerted effort to seek out African Americans and offer them employment.

Over the next few years, under Johnson and his successor, Richard Nixon, the federal government became more and more insistent in its efforts to provide preferential treatment for minorities, particularly blacks. In 1971, for example, the Department of Labor placed a new requirement on contractors—companies that did business with the federal government. To get a federal contract, the order read, these businesses had to employ a reasonable number of racial minorities and women. Companies that did not were told to develop "an acceptable affirmative action program" with "goals and timetables to which the contractor's good faith efforts must be directed to correct the deficiencies."[78]

President Lyndon Johnson, shown here signing the Civil Rights Act of 1968, was a champion of affirmative action.

## Controversy

These directives were controversial. Many political officials and black leaders applauded the government's new commitment to undoing racial discrimination. Others, however, pointed out that simply raising the number of African Americans hired did not always bring about much real change. Communications company AT&T hired hundreds of black workers between the 1940s and the late 1960s. But most of these workers, a government agency pointed out, were telephone operators. These operators —most of them women—held what the agency called "a *horrendous* job," marked by low pay, little respect, and poor working conditions. AT&T could have chosen to "restructure the job, improve the wages, and provide important new avenues for promotion and transfer," the agency asserted, but instead it "decided to keep the wages depressed and simply hire more and more black females."[79]

Proponents of affirmative action soon began turning to the courts for help. They sued to expand affirmative action programs or to force companies and schools to put them in place. The federal government took AT&T to court in 1971, for example, to require the company to offer extra opportunities to blacks and women. After testimony from both sides, a federal judge ruled in favor of the government in 1973. He ordered AT&T to pay damages to its female and African American workers for discriminating against them in the past. And he mandated that the company start hiring and promoting blacks and women "at a pace beyond that which would occur normally."[80]

In the next few years, lawsuits such as these—along with a genuine commitment on the part of many government and business leaders to overcoming the problems of racism—helped spread affirmative action programs throughout both the public and private sectors. Colleges and universities relaxed admissions standards for applicants who were black; local governments and large corporations sought new hires who were women or racial minorities. Some of these policies were quota systems, in which a certain number of jobs or admission slots were reserved for minorities only, while others allowed employers or universities some leeway.

# Criteria for Consideration?

———■———

Whites who are denied jobs or graduate school admissions often focus on the effects of affirmative action, but the situation is usually not quite so simple. Preferences in admissions and hiring, for one thing, are not always based on race. Many colleges give special consideration to athletes, for example, and to the children of alumni. According to one study of Harvard University's admissions policies, alumni children are about three times more likely to be admitted to the school than an applicant with no family ties. White applicants who are turned down for a job or denied admission to a school may have been victimized by these policies just as much as by racial preferences—but they most often blame race for their disappointments.

The reality, too, is that whites compete not only with racial minorities, but with other whites as well. Sometimes, being denied a certain job or admission to graduate school is simply a reflection of supply and demand. Law professor Derrick Bell writes of white students convinced that they were denied admission to Harvard Law School strictly because of that school's racial preferences. "I would point out that the Harvard Law School received up to ten thousand applications from students, at least a third of whom presented records indicating that they could do the work," Bell writes, "but [that] the law school's first-year class was limited to about 550 students." In Bell's opinion, however, his explanation of the odds rarely changed the students' opinions.

Derrick Bell, *Silent Covenants*. New York: Oxford University Press, 2004, p. 143.

These policies, for the most part, did what they promised: They offered minorities a new and more direct path into society. But as affirmative action created greater opportunities for blacks and for other minorities, it inevitably limited opportunities for whites, especially white males. As a result, whites often blamed affirmative action when they were turned down for jobs, denied admission to graduate schools, or passed over for promotions. In their zeal to undo earlier wrongs, these whites charged, those who established affirmative action policies were trampling on the rights of innocent Americans—and unfairly discriminating against people based solely on the color of their skin.

## The *Bakke* Case

As more and more whites found themselves denied the opportunities they wanted, some began turning to the courts for help. The most famous of these cases was brought by a white man named Allan Bakke. In 1972 Bakke applied to the medical school at the University of California at Davis. At the time, this medical school had a two-track system for admission. School officials admitted one hundred students a year, but sixteen of the places

Allan Bakke won the historic reverse discrimination case that overturned some school admission policies based on race quotas.

were reserved for racial minorities under a special program. Since Bakke was white, he was ineligible for this program. In effect, he needed to be one of the top eighty-four students, not one of the top one hundred, in order to get into the school.

Though his qualifications were strong, Bakke was not among the top applicants. He applied again the following year and was turned down once more. Bakke blamed the school's affirmative action policy for these rejections. He noted that most of the minority students accepted into the school had grades and test scores well below his own. As Bakke saw it, he should have been among those accepted; the special program, in his view, was discriminatory and unfair. Accordingly, he sued the medical school, basing his argument on the Fourteenth Amendment and its guarantee of equal protection regardless of race. "I realize that the rationale for these quotas is that they attempt to atone for past racial discrimination," he argued, "but insisting on a new racial bias in favor of minorities is not a just situation."[81]

The first court to hear the case accepted Bakke's argument. The university appealed, however, and the case went to the California Supreme Court. This court upheld the lower court's decision. The Fourteenth Amendment, the judges ruled, was "incompatible with the premise that some races may be afforded a higher degree of protection against unequal treatment than others."[82] By extending unequal treatment to blacks and other minorities, the judges continued, the medical school's admissions program was guilty of discrimination based on race—a clear violation of the Constitution.

University officials appealed once more, and the case moved on to the U.S. Supreme Court. College administrators, politicians, and reporters watched the case quite closely. Many Americans approved of Bakke's argument and hoped the Supreme Court would uphold the earlier rulings. Quite a few labor unions and ethnic organizations, for example, weighed in on Bakke's side. It made little sense, noted the leaders of one of these groups, for "a society trying to rid itself of racial discrimination" to try to "achieve equality . . . by practicing still more racial discrimination."[83]

But others strongly opposed the lawsuit. To some black leaders in particular, the *Bakke* case seemed a perversion of the ideals of the Fourteenth Amendment. This amendment, they argued, needed to be understood in its historical context. It had been designed to lift

# The *Bakke* Decision

———◼———

This is an excerpt from the Supreme Court's decision in the Allan Bakke case. The opinion was written by Justice Lewis Powell. This passage explains Powell's view of how race can legally be considered by a college admissions office.

> Race or ethnic background may be deemed a "plus" in a particular applicant's file, yet it does not insulate the individual from comparison with all other candidates for the available seats. The file of a particular black applicant may be examined for his potential contribution to diversity without the factor of race being decisive when compared, for example, with that of an applicant identified as an Italian-American if the latter is thought to exhibit qualities more likely to promote beneficial educational pluralism [that is, to bring diversity to the school]. Such qualities could include exceptional personal talents, unique work or service experience, leadership potential, maturity, demonstrated compassion, a history of overcoming disadvantage, ability to communicate with the poor, or other qualifications deemed important.

Quoted in Maureen Harrison and Steve Gilbert, *Great Decisions of the U.S. Supreme Court*. New York: Excellent Books, 2003, p. 240.

an oppressed people economically and politically. Since the struggle for civil rights was by no means over, many black leaders believed that the amendment should apply only to those who had truly been disadvantaged. Whites, in this view, simply did not qualify. Thus, many Americans were outraged by Bakke's use of the Fourteenth Amendment to make his case. "The *Bakke* case," said political leader Andrew Young, "is perceived as a betrayal of the black community [on the part of] the judicial system."[84]

## A Decision

The Court began hearing arguments in the *Bakke* case in 1977. The university argued that the special program was needed. Lawyers for the medical school claimed that it was reasonable to

Demonstrators protest the ruling in the *Bakke* court case.

consider race in admission decisions, partly because making up for earlier discrimination was a worthwhile goal and partly because they believed that a school should have the right to choose its students as it wished. They also argued that minority doctors were more likely to set up practices in underserved areas, making the affirmative action policy helpful to society as a whole. Finally, the lawyers argued, the Fourteenth Amendment did not apply to this situation. As affirmative action supporters pointed out, the amendment was designed to safeguard the rights of those who needed help—not middle-class whites.

Bakke's lawyers countered with the argument that any use of race in admission decisions violated the letter of the Constitution. The law was clear, they insisted. Everyone deserved equal protection, with no exceptions. However, the university's policies did not extend the same rights to every applicant. Bakke's legal team asked the Court to require the medical school to admit Bakke as a student and to dismantle the special program that gave minority students an extra edge.

After considerable discussion, the court issued a complicated ruling. Four justices—including Thurgood Marshall, who had argued *Brown v. Board of Education* over twenty years earlier— accepted the university's entire argument. In their minds, affirmative action was completely appropriate, regardless of what form it took and regardless of its effect on whites such as Bakke. Four other justices, in contrast, sided with Bakke. They voted to outlaw all forms of affirmative action for a government-supported school such as the University of California at Davis.

That left one justice, Lewis Powell. Powell took a mixed view of the case; and because his opinion straddled both sides, his view became the official view of the court. First, Powell decided that quotas were not acceptable. By mandating a certain number of minority students, he said, the Davis medical school did indeed unfairly discriminate against Bakke and other whites because of their race. Powell ordered that Bakke be admitted to medical school.

That part of Powell's ruling was a major victory for Bakke. The quota system had been struck down, and Bakke was headed for a medical career after all. But Powell was not done. Switching sides, Powell ruled that while hard-and-fast quotas were unacceptable, the university could *consider* race in admissions decisions. The key, Powell wrote, was whether "race or ethnic background is simply one element—to be weighed fairly against other elements—in the selection process."[85] If it were only one element, a so-called "plus factor," then race could be a consideration.

## The *Weber* Case

The *Bakke* decision, though it drew from ideas on both sides of the debate, was far from the last word on the subject of affirmative action. Unlike cases such as *Brown* or *Plessy v. Ferguson*, in which all or nearly all the justices had agreed, the Court in the *Bakke* case did not speak with one voice. Thus, another court might rule very differently on an almost identical case. Nor was Powell's meaning clear when he said that race could be "one element" of an admissions decision. Reasonable people could well differ about what those words implied. And no one knew whether the ruling might also apply to government employers, private colleges, or businesses.

As a result, the *Bakke* case was followed by many others, most of them filed by white people who, like Bakke, believed that affirmative action policies had unfairly kept them from jobs, promotions, or university admissions. One of the first of these was the case of *United Steelworkers of America v. Weber*, which hinged on an agreement between a labor union and a Louisiana manufacturer. This company hired workers for both skilled and unskilled positions in its factories. The skilled workers were better paid. They were also almost invariably white. In the meantime, the blacks who worked at the factory generally worked in lower-paid jobs.

In the early 1970s union officials and plant managers both wanted to increase the number of blacks who held skilled jobs. Accordingly, the factory established an affirmative action program to raise the proportion of blacks among these workers. The only way for most workers to advance to these positions was by going through a training program. So, the union and the factory managers decided to reserve half of the slots in the program for African Americans. This policy did encourage blacks to enter the training program, but it angered many white workers who felt that they were being unfairly discriminated against by the company and the union.

One of the workers rejected for the training program was a white man named Brian Weber. Weber sued the union for agreeing to permit racial preferences. Weber argued that he had more seniority, or years worked at the plant, than several of the blacks who were admitted to the training program. He added that seniority was commonly used in factories and other workplaces as a main consideration in promotion decisions. Thus, he had been unfairly passed over when the training program was being filled. Lower courts agreed, and the case soon came to the Supreme Court.

After much debate, the Court ruled against Weber. The Court's decision acknowledged the right of private companies to adopt any kind of affirmative action program they wished. The justices, however, were sharply divided. And those who favored Weber's argument were quite pointed in their condemnation of the majority's decision. "There is perhaps no device more destructive to the notion of equality than . . . the quota," wrote Justice William Rehnquist in his dissent. Racial quotas, he added, were "a two-edged sword that must demean one [group] in order to prefer another."[86] In Rehnquist's mind, the ruling permitted and encouraged racial discrimination, which he believed was no less evil when aimed at whites than it was when its victims were African Americans.

## Changing Views in the Court

Rehnquist's position soon became more popular among his colleagues. In 1980 President Ronald Reagan was elected to office. Reagan was not inclined to support affirmative action, and the justices he named to the Supreme Court agreed with him. The 1986 case known as *Wygant v. Board of Education* was a good example of the changing views of the Court. This case dealt with a New Jersey school district that needed to lay off a number of teachers. The district wanted to use race as a factor in determining who should be laid off; school officials were concerned that a strict seniority system would cause the district to lose too many African American teachers. The Court, however, disagreed. Interpreting the Fourteenth Amendment as barring racial discrimination of any kind, the justices required the district to select the teachers strictly according to their seniority.

A 1989 case called *City of Richmond v. J.A. Croson Company* also resulted in a decision against affirmative action. City officials in

Toward the end of the twentieth century, the Supreme Court increasingly ruled against affirmative action initiatives.

Richmond, Virginia, passed a law stating that a percentage of the money the city spent on construction had to go to businesses owned by blacks or other racial minorities. A white-owned company sued the city, hoping to overturn the law. In a split decision, the Supreme Court ruled that the law was wrong. A few justices used the opportunity to express their disapproval of affirmative action in general. Support of racial preferences, said Justice Antonin Scalia, represents "a manner of thinking by race that was the source of the injustice and that will, if it endures within our society, be the source of more injustice still."[87]

With the Supreme Court becoming more and more willing to reject racial preferences, whites angry about laws and policies that favored blacks increasingly turned to the judicial system for help. For the most part, they got favorable rulings. In *Martin v. Wilks*, a 1989 case, the Supreme Court threw out a 1974 decision by a lower court that the city of Birmingham, Alabama, had to use affirmative action to increase the number of black firefighters. In a 1995 case known as *Adarand v. Peña*, the Supreme Court ruled that the federal government could establish affirmative action policies but only in limited and temporary situations. And in *Hopwood v. Texas*, decided in 1996, an appeals court required the University of Texas Law School to stop using racial preferences in its admission process.

Many observers applauded these rulings. Others, however, were alarmed at the trend of the courts—and at the reasoning given in some of the decisions. In *Hopwood*, for example, writes a commentator, "the judges discounted the infamous history of the University of Texas Law School, stretching back to the case of Herman Sweatt [who had been denied admission to the school in 1950 on racial grounds] and continuing into at least the 1970s."[88] And Supreme Court justice Harry Blackmun, a staunch supporter of affirmative action, wrote in frustration after dissenting from yet another decision, "One wonders whether the majority still believes that race discrimination [against nonwhites] is a problem in our society, or even remembers that it ever was."[89]

## The Twenty-First Century

The affirmative action court cases of the early 2000s, like earlier cases, have been closely watched, hard fought, and highly controversial. Most have also been decided by narrow majorities. In 2003, for example, the Supreme Court heard two very similar cases at once, both involving the University of Michigan. The case *Gratz v. Bollinger* dealt with a white high school student denied admission to the college. The companion case, *Grutter v. Bollinger*, dealt with a white woman who had been rejected by the university's law school. In each case, the rejected student sued the college to force an end to racial preferences of any kind. Both cases were decided by a slender 5–4 majority. But as if to underscore the degree of disagreement among members of the Court, the justices ruled in favor of the plaintiff in *Gratz* while upholding the university's affirmative action program in *Grutter*.

Another more recent example comes from 2007. Hoping to achieve racial balance in district high schools, the school systems

Barbara Grutter (left) and Jennifer Gratz (right) were plaintiffs in two high-profile affirmative action cases before the Supreme Court.

in Seattle, Washington, and Louisville, Kentucky, used race as a factor in determining which students would attend which schools. Some white parents complained, however, alleging that their children were unfairly denied admission to the high schools of their choice because of their race. Chief Justice John Roberts agreed. "The way to stop discrimination on the basis of race," he wrote pointedly, "is to stop discriminating on the basis of race."[90] But half his colleagues strongly disagreed. In yet another split, the Court ruled 5–4 for the plaintiffs.

Clearly, the battle over affirmative action, both in and out of the court system, is far from over. Neither judges nor ordinary citizens have reached a consensus about whether racial preferences are ever acceptable—and if they are, what they may look like and under what circumstances they may be used. The *Bakke* decision was merely the first in a long line of split decisions. It is doubtful that the Seattle and Louisville cases will be the last.

What the future may hold is anyone's guess. But certainly, all Americans can agree with the ideal expressed by Justice Sandra Day O'Connor in her opinion on the University of Michigan cases. Noting the remarkable gains by African Americans and other racial minorities over the years, and noting as well the increasing tolerance and acceptance among people of different races, O'Connor wrote: "We expect that 25 years from now the use of racial preferences will no longer be necessary to further the interest approved today."[91]

# Notes

## Chapter One: The *Dred Scott* Decision

1. Quoted in David Brion Davis and Steven Mintz, *The Boisterous Sea of Liberty: A Documentary History of America from Discovery Through the Civil War*. New York: Oxford University Press, 1998, p. 58.

2. Quoted in Paul Finkelman, *Slavery and the Founders*. New York: M.E. Sharpe, 2001, p. 75.

3. Quoted in David P. Currie, *The Constitution in the Supreme Court, 1789–1888*. Chicago: University of Chicago Press, 1985, p. 263.

4. Quoted in Missouri Digital Heritage, "Laws of the State of Missouri: Freedom." www.sos.mo.gov/archives/education/aahi/beforedredscott/1824Missouri Law.asp.

5. Luther S. Cushing, *American Jurist and Law Magazine*, vol. 4. Boston: Charles C. Little and James Brown, 1843, p. 447.

6. Gregory J. Wallance, "*Dred Scott* Decision: The Lawsuit That Started the Civil War," *Civil War Times*, March/April 2006. www.historynet.com/dred-scott-decision-the-lawsuit-that-started-the-civil-war.htm.

7. Quoted in Wallance, "*Dred Scott* Decision: The Lawsuit That Started the Civil War."

8. Quoted in James Oliver Horton, ed., *Landmarks of African American History*. New York: Oxford University Press, 2005, p. 63.

9. Quoted in Paul Finkelman, Dred Scott v. Sandford: *A Brief History with Documents*. New York: Macmillan, 1997, p. 22.

10. Quoted in Finkelman, Dred Scott v. Sandford: *A Brief History with Documents*, p. 25.

11. Quoted in Kenneth C. Kaufman, *Dred Scott's Advocate: A Biography of Roswell M. Field*. Columbia: University of Missouri Press, 1996, p. 223.

12. Quoted in Cornell University Law School, "United States Constitution: Article IV." www.law.cornell.edu/constitution/constitution.articleiv.html.

13. Quoted in Maureen Harrison and Steve Gilbert, eds., *Great*

*Decisions of the U.S. Supreme Court*. New York: Excellent Books, 2003, p. 18.

14. Quoted in Mark A. Graber, Dred Scott *and the Problem of Constitutional Evil*. New York: Cambridge University Press, 2006, p. 68.

15. Quoted in Harrison and Gilbert, *Great Decisions of the U.S. Supreme Court*, p. 32.

16. Quoted in Horton, *Landmarks of African American History*, p. 69.

17. Quoted in Mary Ann Harrell, *Equal Justice Under the Law*. Washington, DC: Supreme Court Historical Society, 1982, p. 43.

18. Quoted in Lewis Copeland, Lawrence W. Lamm, and Stephen J. McKenna, eds., *The World's Great Speeches*. New York: Courier Dover, 1999, p. 313.

19. Quoted in Henry Mayer, *All on Fire: William Lloyd Garrison and the Abolition of Slavery*. New York: St. Martin's, 1998, p. 439.

20. Quoted in Wallance, "*Dred Scott* Decision: The Lawsuit That Started the Civil War."

**Chapter Two: *Plessy v. Ferguson***
21. Quoted in Cornell University Law School, "United States Constitution: Amendment XIII." www.law.cornell.edu constitution/constitution.amend mentxiii.html.

22. Quoted in Eric McKitrick, ed., *Slavery Defended: The Views of the Old South*. Englewood Cliffs, NJ: Prentice-Hall, 1963, p. 9.

23. Quoted in Keith Weldon Medley, *We as Freemen*. Gretna, LA: Pelican, 2003, p. 60.

24. Quoted in Noralee Frankel, *Break Those Chains at Last*. New York: Oxford University Press, 1996, p. 22.

25. Quoted in William H. Chafe, ed., *Remembering Jim Crow*. New York: New Press, 2001, p. 44.

26. Quoted in Cornell University Law School, "United States Constitution: Amendment XIV." www.law.cornell.edu/ constitution/constitution .amendmentxiv.html.

27. Quoted in Harvey Fireside, *Separate and Unequal*. New York: Carroll and Graf, 2004, p. 63.

28. Quoted in Harrison and Gilbert, *Great Decisions of the U.S. Supreme Court*, p. 33.

29. Quoted in Chafe, *Remembering Jim Crow*, p. 72.

30. Quoted in Medley, *We as Freemen*, p. 96.

31. Quoted in Charles A. Lofgren, *The Plessy Case: A Legal-Historical Interpretation*. New York: Oxford University Press, 1987, p. 12.

32. Quoted in Medley, *We as Freemen*, p. 89.

33. Quoted in Fireside, *Separate and Unequal*, p. 1.

34. Quoted in Medley, *We as Freemen*, p. 142.

35. Quoted in Medley, *We as Freemen*, p. 162.

36. Quoted in Medley, *We as Freemen*, p. 201.

37. Quoted in Harrison and Gilbert, *Great Decisions of the U.S. Supreme Court*, p. 33.

38. Quoted in Harrison and Gilbert, *Great Decisions of the U.S. Supreme Court*, p. 43.

39. Quoted in Harrison and Gilbert, *Great Decisions of the U.S. Supreme Court*, pp. 44–45.

40. Quoted in Fireside, *Separate and Unequal*, p. 217.

41. Fireside, *Separate and Unequal*, title page.

**Chapter Three: *Brown v. Board of Education***

42. Quoted in Diane Telgen, *Defining Moments:* Brown v. Board of Education. Detroit: Omnigraphics, 2005, p. 3.

43. Quoted in Derrick Bell, *Silent Covenants*. New York: Oxford University Press, 2004, p. 23.

44. Quoted in Telgen, *Defining Moments:* Brown v. Board of Education, p. 25.

45. Quoted in Telgen, *Defining Moments:* Brown v. Board of Education, p. 34.

46. Quoted in Fireside, *Separate and Unequal*, p. 290.

47. Quoted in Fireside, *Separate and Unequal*, pp. 293–94.

48. Quoted in Telgen, *Defining Moments:* Brown v. Board of Education, p. 39.

49. Quoted in Telgen, *Defining Moments:* Brown v. Board of Education, p. 133.

50. Quoted in Fireside, *Separate and Unequal*, p. 297.

51. Quoted in Harrison and Gilbert, *Great Decisions of the U.S. Supreme Court*, p. 73.

52. Quoted in Horton, *Landmarks of African American History*, p. 174.

53. Quoted in Bell, *Silent Covenants*, p. 17.

54. Quoted in Harrison and Gilbert, *Great Decisions of the U.S. Supreme Court*, p. 78.

55. Quoted in Telgen, *Defining Moments:* Brown v. Board of Education, p. 71.

56. Quoted in Fireside, *Separate and Unequal*, p. 309.

57. Quoted in Fireside, *Separate and Unequal*, p. 300.

**Chapter Four: Voting Rights and Political Power**

58. Quoted in William Dudley, ed., *Slavery: Opposing Viewpoints.* San Diego: Greenhaven, 1992, p. 206.

59. Quoted in Cornell University Law School, "United States Constitution: Amendment XV." www.law.cornell.edu/constitution/constitution.amendmentxv.html.

60. Henry Hampton and Steve Fayer, *Voices of Freedom.* New York: Bantam, 1990, p. 2.

61. Quoted in *New Georgia Encyclopedia*, "History and Archaeology." www.georgiaencyclopedia.org/nge/Article.jsp?id=h-1097.

62. Quoted in "Guinn v. United States, *Further Readings*," in *American Law and Legal Information: Great American Court Cases,* vol. 15. http://law.jrank.org/pages/13382/Guinn-v-United-States.html.

63. Quoted in *Veterans of the Civil Rights Movement*, "Voting Rights: Alabama Literacy Test." www.crmvet.org/info/lithome.htm.

64. Quoted in Hampton and Fayer, *Voices of Freedom*, pp. 178–79.

65. Quoted in blackpast.org, "*Guinn v. United States:* The Grandfather Clause (1915)." www.blackpast.org/?q=primarywest/guinn-v-united-states-grandfather-clause-1915.

66. Quoted in Richard A. Posner, ed., *The Essential Holmes.* Chicago: University of Chicago Press, 1997, p. 154.

67. Quoted in Fireside, *Separate and Unequal*, p. 254.

68. Quoted in blackpast.org, "*Gomillion v. Lightfoot, Mayor of Tuskegee.*" www.blackpast.org/?q=primary/gomillion-v-lightfoot-mayor-tuskegee.

69. Quoted in blackpast.org, "*Gomillion v. Lightfoot, Mayor of Tuskegee.*"

70. Quoted in Tulane University Special Collections, "Louisiana Political Ephemera in the Special Collections Vertical Files: One-Third Democracy for One-Sixth of the Nation." http://specialcollections.tulane.edu/PolyEph/Poll.htm.

71. Quoted in Cornell University Law School, Supreme Court Collection, "*Harper v. Virginia Board of Elections.*" www.law.cornell.edu/supct/html/historics/USSC_CR_0383_0663_ZO.html.

72. Ourdocuments.gov, "Transcript of Voting Rights Act (1965)." www.ourdocuments.gov/doc.php?flash=true&doc=100&page=transcript.

73. Ourdocuments.gov, "Transcript of Voting Rights Act (1965)."

74. Quoted in Cornell University

Law School, Supreme Court Collection, "*South Carolina v. Katzenbach*," www.law.cornell.edu/supct/html/historics/USSC_CR_0383_0301_ZS.html.

## Chapter Five: Affirmative Action

75. Quoted in Jo Ann Ooiman Robinson, ed., *Affirmative Action: A Documentary History*. Westport, CT: Greenwood, 2001, pp. 49–50.

76. Quoted in Terry H. Anderson, *The Pursuit of Fairness*. New York: Oxford University Press, 2004, p. 88.

77. Quoted in Steven M. Cahn, ed., *The Affirmative Action Debate*, 2nd ed. New York: Routledge, 2002, p. xii.

78. Quoted in Cahn, *The Affirmative Action Debate*, p. xii.

79. Quoted in Robinson, *Affirmative Action: A Documentary History*, p. 178.

80. Quoted in Robinson, *Affirmative Action: A Documentary History*, p. 181.

81. Quoted in Anderson, *The Pursuit of Fairness*, p. 152.

82. Quoted in Anderson, *The Pursuit of Fairness*, p. 153.

83. Quoted in Anderson, *The Pursuit of Fairness*, p. 153.

84. Quoted in Robinson, *Affirmative Action: A Documentary History*, p. 204.

85. Quoted in Anderson, *The Pursuit of Fairness*, p. 155.

86. Quoted in Robinson, *Affirmative Action: A Documentary History*, p. 235.

87. Quoted in Robinson, *Affirmative Action: A Documentary History*, p. 291.

88. Robinson, *Affirmative Action: A Documentary History*, p. 331.

89. Quoted in Robinson, *Affirmative Action: A Documentary History*, p. 296.

90. Quoted in Jessica Blanchard and Christine Frey, "Schools Seek New Diversity Answers After Court Rejects Tiebreaker," *Seattle Post-Intelligencer*, June 7, 2007. http://seattlepi.nwsource.com/local/321632_race29.html.

91. Quoted in Fireside, *Separate and Unequal*, pp. 328–29.

# For More Information

## Books

Nathan Aaseng, Plessy v. Ferguson: *Separate but Equal.* San Diego: Lucent, 2003. An account of the proceedings and the issues involved in the *Plessy* case that established the principle of "separate but equal."

Harvey Fireside, *Separate and Unequal.* New York: Carroll and Graf, 2004. Nicely written and always interesting, this book focuses on the *Plessy v. Ferguson* case but provides information on several other court cases as well.

Susan Dudley Gold, Brown v. Board of Education: *Separate but Equal?* New York: Benchmark, 2005. An interesting and well-researched discussion of the *Brown* case and its aftermath.

Mary Ann Harrell, *Equal Justice Under the Law.* Washington, DC: Supreme Court Historical Society, 1982. A richly illustrated account of important cases heard by the U.S. Supreme Court through the years. Includes information on several of the cases mentioned in this book.

Maureen Harrison and Steve Gilbert, eds., *Great Decisions of the U.S.*

*Supreme Court.* New York: Excellent Books, 2003. Excerpts from the Supreme Court rulings in sixteen important cases, including *Dred Scott, Plessy v. Ferguson, Brown v. Board of Education*, and the *Bakke* case. Some excerpts from dissenting opinions are given as well, notably in the *Plessy* case.

James Oliver Horton, ed., *Landmarks of African American History.* New York: Oxford University Press, 2005. A guide to historical landmarks that bear a connection to the black experience. Includes information on the St. Louis Courthouse and Dred Scott, along with the *Brown v. Board of Education* National Historic Site in Kansas.

Bonnie Lukes, *The* Dred Scott *Decision.* San Diego: Lucent, 1997. About the *Dred Scott* case. A well-written account of the history and the trial.

Tim McNeese, Dred Scott v. Sandford: *The Pursuit of Freedom.* New York: Chelsea House, 2007. A well-researched and clear discussion of the *Dred Scott* decision, including important background information on slavery.

————, Plessy v. Ferguson: *Separate but Equal*. New York: Chelsea House, 2007. Describes the *Plessy* case, including information on Louisiana, black-white relations, and Jim Crow laws.

Jo Ann Ooiman Robinson, ed., *Affirmative Action: A Documentary History*. Westport, CT: Greenwood, 2001. A collection of primary source documents relating to affirmative action as it has pertained to race, gender, and disability over the years. Includes useful commentary, which provides background and context for the documents.

Rebecca Stefoff, *The Bakke Case*. New York: Benchmark, 2006. Discusses the *Bakke* case, placing it in the context of other affirmative action decisions and other cases and laws that involved the status of African Americans.

James Tackach, *Famous Trials:* Brown v. Board of Education. San Diego: Lucent, 1998. An account of the case that resulted in the end of segregation.

Diane Telgen, *Defining Moments:* Brown v. Board of Education. Detroit: Omnigraphics, 2005. Thoroughly researched, with plenty of background about the *Brown* case. Includes biographical information on many of the participants in the trial and a number of primary source documents.

## DVDs

*Africans in America: America's Journey Through Slavery*. DVD. WBGH Boston, 1998. This film provides valuable background information about slavery as well as information about the *Dred Scott* case.

*The History Channel Presents Voices of Civil Rights*. DVD. History Channel, 2007. A series of documentaries about the civil rights movement, focusing on both the leaders of the movement and the experiences of ordinary black Americans.

*In the Land of Jim Crow: Growing Up Segregated*. DVD. Phoenix Learning, 2008. A film about life in the South in the early 1900s, with information about segregation and the *Plessy* and *Brown* cases.

*In the Land of Jim Crow: Using the Vote, Sharing Power*. DVD. Phoenix Learning, 2008. This film is about the Jim Crow era and its passing, including information on voting rights.

*Thurgood Marshall: Justice for All*. DVD. Biography Channel, 2005. A profile of the NAACP lawyer and Supreme Court justice, with information on *Brown v. Board of Education* along with voting rights cases and affirmative action decisions.

*With All Deliberate Speed.* DVD. Starz/Anchor Bay, 2005. A film about the *Brown* case and the desegregation of schools.

## Web Sites

**Brown Foundation for Educational Equity: "*Brown v. Board of Education:* About the Case"** (http://brownvboard.org/summary/). This Web site contains links and information having to do with the *Brown* decision.

**Ourdocuments.org: "100 Milestone Documents"** (www.ourdocuments .gov/content.php?page=mile stone). This Web site includes the text of many important documents through American history, including documents connected to several of the cases in this book.

**PBS: "Africans in America: Dred Scott's Fight for Freedom"** (www .pbs.org/wgbh/aia/part4/4p2932.ht ml). This Web page about the *Dred Scott* case also includes background on slavery and the law.

**Street Law and the Supreme Court Historical Society: "Landmark Cases"** (www.landmarkcases.org/). Includes information on *Plessy v. Ferguson*, *Scott v. Sandford*, and other cases of particular importance to African Americans.

# Index

A

*Adarand v. Peña* (1995), 88

Affirmative action

  *Bakke* decision, 84–85

  controversy over, 74

  early examples of, 75–76

  Supreme Court's changing view on, 86, 88–90

  *Weber* decision, 86

  white opposition to, 79

AT&T, 78

B

Bakke, Allan, 80, *80*

Bell, Derrick, 60, 79

*Belton, Gebhart v.* (DE, 1952), 49

Black Codes, 27–29

  in Louisiana, 28

Blackmun, Harry, 88

*Board of Education, Brown v. See Brown v. Board of Education*

*Board of Education, Wygant v.* (1986), 86

*Bollinger, Gratz v.* (2003), 89

*Bollinger, Grutter v.* (2003), 89

*Breedlove v. Suttles* (1937), 66, 69

*Briggs v. Elliott* (SC, 1952), 49, 50

Brown, Henry, 38, *38*, 40

Brown, Linda, 50

Brown, Oliver, 50

*Brown II* (1955), 55–56

*Brown v. Board of Education* (1954), 50

  arguments in, 51–53

  plaintiffs in, *51*

  reaction to, 55

  ruling in, 53–55

Bryan, William Jennings, 34

C

Calhoun, John, 27

Carter, Joe, *63*

Child, Lydia Maria, 61

*City of Richmond v. J.A. Croson Company* (1989), 86–87, 88

Civil Rights Act (1965), 71–72

Civil rights movement, 59, 68

  successes of, 41–42

Clark, Kenneth, 51, *52*

Constitution. *See* U.S. Constitution

Court system, 8–9

Curtis, Benjamin, 21–22

D

Darrow, Clarence, 34

Department of Labor, U.S., 76

Doar, John, 72

Douglass, Frederick, 22

*Dred Scott* decision (1857), 20–22

  effects of, 24

  modern scholars' views on, 23

  reaction to, 22–24

DuBois, W.E.B., 44, 50

E

*Elliott, Briggs v.* (SC, 1952), 49, 50

Emerson, Irene, 14–15, 17, 18

Emerson, John, 11–12, 13
Emerson, John, Jr., 18
Engelhardt, Samuel, 70

F
Ferguson, John, 35
Ferguson, Plessy v. See Plessy v.
  Ferguson
Fifteenth Amendment (1870), 62,
  66, 73
Fourteenth Amendment (1868),
  29–30, 35
  in Bakke case, 81–82
  in Brown case, 53, 54–55
  in Plessy case, 36
Frankfurter, Felix, 69

G
Gaines, Lloyd, 46
Gebhart v. Belton (Delaware, 1952),
  49
Gerrymandering, 69
Giles v. Harris (1903), 67
Gomillion v. Lightfoot (1960), 68–69,
  73
Grandfather clause, 64–65
Gratz, Jennifer, 89
Gratz v. Bollinger (2003), 89
Grutter, Barbara, 89
Grutter v. Bollinger (2003), 89
Guinn v. United States (1915), 66–67,
  73

H
Harlan, John, 36, 39, 39, 40
Harper, Annie, 69, 71
Harper v. Virginia Board of Elections
  (1966), 69, 73

Harris, Giles v. (1903), 67
Herndon, Nixon v. (1927), 67–68, 73
Holmes, Oliver Wendell, 67, 71
Hopwood v. Texas (1996), 88

J
J.A. Croson Company, City of Richmond
  v. (1989), 86–87, 88
Jefferson, Thomas, 13
Jim Crow laws, 25, 30–31
Johnson, Lyndon B., 57, 69, 77
  affirmative action and, 76
Judicial system, 7, 8

K
Katzenbach, Nicholas, 72
Katzenbach, South Carolina v. (1966),
  73
Kennedy, John F., 76
King, Martin Luther, Jr., 42

L
Lee, George, 62
Lightfoot, Gomillion v. (1960), 68–69,
  73
Literacy tests, 64, 65
  banning of, 72
Little Rock (AR), desegregation of
  Central High School (1957), 57
Louisiana, 28

M
Marshall, Thurgood, 45, 50, 58, 72, 84
  in Murray case, 45, 46
Martin v. Wilks (1989), 88
McLaurin, George, 48
McLaurin v. Oklahoma State Regents
  (1950), 48

*Melvin, Wilson v.* (1837), 15
Missouri Compromise (1820), *12, 13*
Murray, Donald, 44–46

N
National Association for the
  Advancement of Colored People
  (NAACP), 45, 49, 53
Nixon, Richard, 76
*Nixon v. Herndon* (1927), 67–68, 73

O
O'Connor, Sandra Day, 90
*Oklahoma State Regents, McLaurin v.*
  (1950), 48

P
*Painter, Sweatt v.* (1950), 46–47
Parks, Rosa, 42
Pattillo, Melba, 57
*Peña, Adarand v.* (1995), 88
Plessy, Homer, 34–35
*Plessy v. Ferguson* (1896), 25, 34
  arguments in, 36–37
  Harlan's dissent in, 39
  verdict in, 38, 40
Poll tax, 62–63
  ban on, 69
  exceptions for whites under, 64, 65
Powell, Louis, 82, 84–85

R
Reagan, Ronald, 86
Reconstruction, 30
  black voting rights during, 61–62
Rehnquist, William, 86
Roberts, John, 90

S
*Sandford, Scott v.* (1857), 10, 25
  See also *Dred Scott* decision
Scalia, Antonin, 88
Schools, segregation of, *42–43,* 44
  *Brown II* decision and, 55–56
  challenge of, 49–55
  effects on black children, 51, 54
  graduate students challenge, 44–49
  Johnson, Lyndon, and, 57
Scopes, John T., 34
*Scopes v. Tennessee* (1925), 34
Scott, Dred, 10, 11, *11,* 12, 14–15
Scott, Harriet (Robinson), 10, 14
Scott, William, 18
*Scott v. Sandford* (1857), 10, 25
  See also *Dred Scott* decision
Segregation, 30–31
  effects of *Plessy* decision on, 40
  Warren, Earl, on, 54
  *See also* Schools, segregation of
Separate Car Act (LA, 1890), 32–33,
  36
  upholding of, 40
Separate-but-equal doctrine, 46, 47
  overturning of, 54
  view of black leaders on, 50
Slavery
  change in southern view of, 17–18
  *Dred Scott* decision and, 10
  southern justification of, 26–27
*South Carolina v. Katzenbach* (1966),
  73
Supreme Court, 9
  *See also specific decisions*
*Suttles, Breedlove v.* (1937), 66, 69
Sweatt, Herman, 46, *47,* 88
*Sweatt v. Painter* (1950), 46–47

T
Taney, Roger, 21
Taylor, Susie Baker King, 64
Tennessee, Scopes v. (1925), 34
Territories, U.S., 12
  Missouri Compromise and, 13
Texas, Hopwood v. (1996), 88
Thirteenth Amendment (1865), 26
Tourgée, Albion, 36, 37
Tuskegee (AL), redrawing of election
  districts in, 68–69
Twenty-fourth Amendment (1964),
  69, 71

U
United States
  division into free and slave states,
  12, 13
United States, Guinn v. (1915), 66–67,
  73
U.S. Constitution, 7
  See also Thirteenth Amendment;
    Fourteenth Amendment; Fifteenth
    Amendment; Twenty-fourth
    Amendment
United Steelworkers of America v.
  Weber (1979), 85–86

V
Vinson, Fred, 47

Virginia Board of Elections, Harper v.
  (1966), 69, 73
Voting rights
  African Americans demand, 71
  cases, 59-60
  Fifteenth Amendment and, 62
  in post-Reconstruction South,
    62–66
Voting Rights Act (1965), 71–72
  challenge to, 72–73
  current debate over, 73, 75

W
Walker, Rachel v. (1837), 15–16
Waring, J. Waties, 49
Warren, Earl, 53, 53, 54, 73
Weber, Brian, 86
Weber, United Steelworkers of America
  v. (1979), 85–86
Wells, Robert, 19
Whitesides, Winny v. (1824), 15
Wilks, Martin v. (1989), 88
Wilson v. Melvin (1837), 15
Winny v. Whitesides (1824), 15
Wygant v. Board of Education (1986),
  86

Y
Young, Andrew, 82

# Picture Credits

Cover photo: © Bettmann/Corbis
© Bob Adelman/Corbis, 63
AP Images, 89
© Bettmann/Corbis, 26, 42–43, 48, 53, 72, 77, 80, 83
© Charles O. Cecil/Alamy, 14
© David Coleman/Alamy, 8
© Corbis, 38, 45
© Coston Stock/Alamy, 7
Don Cravens/Time Life Pictures/Getty Images, 70
Al Fenn/Time Life Pictures/Getty Images, 17
Getty Images, 51
The Library of Congress, 37, 39, 56
© The London Art Archive/Alamy, 33
© Robert Maass/Corbis, 52
MPI/Hulton Archive/Getty Images, 29
© North Wind Picture Archives/Alamy, 11, 12, 20, 61
Joseph Scherschel/Time Life Pictures/Getty Images, 47
© Jim West/Alamy, 87

# About the Author

Stephen Currie is the author of many books, articles, and educational materials. He has written extensively on African American history, including *The African American Religious Experience*, *Murder in Mississippi*, *African American Folklore*, *Life of a Slave on a Southern Plantation*, and others, all for Lucent Books. He is also a teacher. He lives with his family in New York State's Hudson River valley, where he enjoys kayaking, bicycling, and snowshoeing.